The Kidai Shōran Scroll

This book has been produced "backwards" for a very important reason.
Japanese has traditionally been written vertically from right to left, and the *Kidai Shōran* scroll—the artistic masterpiece that is the subject of this book—was also created to be viewed in that direction. Rather than "reverse engineer" the experience of viewing this scroll for readers, this English translation follows in the footsteps of the Japanese original, and should be read from right to left.

JAPAN LIBRARY

The Kidai Shōran *Scroll*

**TOKYO STREET LIFE
IN THE EDO PERIOD**

Ozawa Hiromu *and*
Kobayashi Tadashi

Translated by Juliet Winters Carpenter

Japan Publishing Industry Foundation for Culture

Table of *Contents*

This book follows the Japanese layout from right to left

Strolling through *Kidai Shōran*
PART I   *14*

Edo Merchants' Roots:
Ise Merchants on the Rise   26

A Merchant's Career Path:
A Rocky Road   27

A Merchant's Life Plan:
The Pleasures of Retirement   28

Merchants on the Road:
The Luxurious Travels of
Lucky Retirees   29

The World of *Kidai Shōran*:
Life in Edo, 200 Years Ago   *6*
by Ozawa Hiromu
The Discovery   6
The Mysteries   7
The Contents   8
Tracing the Scroll's
Chinese Roots   9

Streets and Districts in the
Vicinity of Nihonbashi   10

The Scroll in its Entirety   12

Note to readers
This book follows the Hepburn system of romanization. Except for place names found on international maps, long vowels are indicated by macrons. The tradition of placing the family name first has been followed for Japanese names.

The Kidai Shōran *Scroll: Tokyo Street Life in the Edo Period*
By Ozawa Hiromu and Kobayashi Tadashi.
Translated by Juliet Winters Carpenter.

Published by
Japan Publishing Industry Foundation for Culture (JPIC)
2-2-30 Kanda-Jinbocho, Chiyoda-ku, Tokyo 101-0051, Japan

First English edition: March 2020

© 2006 Ozawa Hiromu and Kobayashi Tadashi
English translation © 2020 Japan Publishing Industry
Foundation for Culture
All rights reserved

This book is a translation of *[Kidai Shōran no Nihonbashi]: Kakki ni afureta Edo no machi* which was originally published by Shogakukan Inc., in 2016.
English publishing rights arranged with Shogakukan Inc.

Kidai Shōran, hand scroll, ink and colours on paper,
43.7 x 1232.2 cm. Japan, Tokugawa period.
© Staatliche Museen zu Berlin, Museum für Asiatische Kunst, former collection of Hans-Joachim and Inge Küster, gift of Manfred Bohms, 2002-17

Book design: Andrew Pothecary (itsumo music)

Printed in Japan
ISBN 978-4-86658-132-3
https://japanlibrary.jpic.or.jp/

**Occupations and Arts
Illustrated in** *Kidai Shōran*   74

A Guided Tour through
Kidai Shōran   86

**More about the
Picture Scroll** *Kidai Shōran*
by Kobayashi Tadashi   96

The Location of the
Kidai Shōran **Scroll**   102

About the Authors   104

About the Translator   104

Strolling through *Kidai Shōran*
PART IV   *56*

Merchants' Amusements:
All-Day Kabuki   72

Merchants' Favorite Reading:
From "How-To" Books to
Digests of Great Works   73

Strolling through *Kidai Shōran*
PART III   *44*

Merchants' Attire:
A Refined Style, Unseen   54

Merchants' Pastimes:
The Fascination with
Horticulture   55

Strolling through *Kidai Shōran*
PART II   *30*

Edo Merchants and Fires:
Disaster as a
Business Opportunity   42

Treating Disease:
Supplements, Massage,
Hot Springs   43

The World of *Kidai Shōran*: Life in Edo, 200 Years Ago

by
Ozawa Hiromu

The Discovery

The scroll painting *Kidai Shōran* (Excellent view of this prosperous age) was found in the attic of a relative by Hans-Joachim Küster, a professor of biology at the Free University of Berlin, and his wife Inge. The Küsters were collectors of Chinese art, and as members of the Society of Friends of the Museum of East Asian Art, Berlin, which is under the purview of the Prussian Cultural Heritage Foundation, they donated the scroll—with the support of Manfred Bohms—along with their entire art collection, to the museum. How the scroll painting made its way to that German house is unknown.

The title is written in Chinese characters, and this apparently caused the painting to be mistaken for a work of Chinese art. After Professor Küster's death in 1995, the scroll lay unnoticed in the museum warehouse until it came to light in an inheritance dispute.

Just around that time, the Dahlem Museum complex, which includes the Museum of East Asian Art, Berlin, was undergoing renovation and enlarging its Japanese art gallery. In need of a work to feature in its reopening, the Museum of East Asian Art, Berlin, chose Dr. Khanh Trinh, a curator of Japanese art, to head the search. She was able to establish that *Kidai Shōran* was not Chinese, but a Japanese work dating to 1805, the second year of the Bunka era. It was a treasure, offering a richly detailed picture of Edo life on the main street between Nihonbashi Bridge and Imagawabashi Bridge.

To verify the details, museum director Dr. Willibald Veit consulted with his friend, Dr. Franziska Ehmcke, a professor of Japanese Studies at the University of Cologne. She in turn consulted with Professor Kobayashi Tadashi of Gakushuin University—and so the scroll was finally reintroduced to its country of origin, Japan.

Kidai Shōran title calligraphy, by Sano Tōshū.

The Mysteries

Kidai Shōran is an illustrated scroll of color painting on paper, 12.3 meters long and 43 centimeters high—much larger than the average scroll painting. Blank end paper takes up 48 centimeters, the title calligraphy 1.26 meters, and the graphic depiction of the street 10.55 meters.

A label on gold paper identifies this as the *ten* ("heaven") volume, suggesting the existence of a *chi* ("earth") volume and possibly a *jin* ("humankind") volume. However, the Küsters' donation to the museum included no other such scrolls. This volume gives an overview of the west side of Nihonbashi Street, near Edo Castle in the capital city of Edo (present-day Tokyo), as seen from the east. The missing volumes might have shown the street from the opposite side, or possibly the section from Nihonbashi to Kyōbashi, or Honchō Street.

The title was brushed in large strokes by Sano Tōshū, a famous Edo calligrapher of the time whose identity is established by two seals. His given name was Jun, and he also painted under the names Kuntaku and Bunsuke; he is known to have died on the tenth day of the third month, 1814. In 1804, around the time this scroll painting came into being, the popular novelist Santō Kyōzan (1769–1858) became Sano's adopted son-in-law, taking the name Ranzan Sano Eisuke (he later severed the connection).

The artist is unknown, there being neither signature nor seal. The leading candidate among people connected with Sano Tōshū is Santō Kyōden (1761–1816), Kyōzan's older brother and, like him, a writer of popular novels. Born Iwase Samuru in Edo's Fukagawa neighborhood, Kyōden was known popularly as Kyōya Denzō. He studied with the ukiyo-e master Kitao Shigemasa (1739–1820) and, under the pseudonym Kitao Masanobu, supplied illustrations for many *kibyōshi* and *gesaku*, two genres of Edo-period popular fiction, besides illustrating his own works.

Kyōden lived in Kyōbashi, where he also ran a tobacco store. He wrote works such as the 1787 *Tsūgen sōmagaki* (How to appear a man of refined taste in the best houses of pleasure), but later ran afoul of the Kansei Reforms (1787–1793), under which decadent writings were condemned. A 1791 trilogy of his was banned, including the very popular work *Shikake bunko* (The trick clothing-box) about the lives of Fukagawa courtesans, and Kyōden was chained to his house in manacles for fifty days as punishment. Later, he wrote essays on Edo customs and mores, such as the 1804 *Kottōshū* (Antique collection) and the 1815 *Kinsei kisekikō* (Extraordinary facts of the present day). Some of his paintings, such as the 1798 *Shiki no yukikai* (The changing seasons), are similar in composition to *Kidai Shōran*.

Kidai Shōran offers a lively depiction of Nihonbashi Street during its Edo-period heyday, and a hint of its date of origin may be found in one of its scenes. Among the people shown marching to solicit donations for the rebuilding of Ekō-in temple, one is carrying a donation box labeled "Ekō-in, Bunka 2." This reference to the second year of the Bunka era may be an indication that the scroll was painted around that year; i.e., 1805.

Along the great street, eighty-eight shops are portrayed, and shop curtains, signs, and banners bear the shop names, trademarks, and other information. A highlight of the painting is the inclusion of official notices outlawing Christianity and the shooting of guns that are posted in the Minamibashi area, dated Shōtoku 1 (1711) and Kyōho 6 (1721). The tiny lettering is all but invisible to the naked eye, but shows up clearly when viewed through a magnifying glass. Through such devices, the artist draws us into the Edo microculture in this miniature recreation of time past.

Original railing decoration of Nihonbashi Bridge, November 1658, cast by Shiina Hyōko. (Photo: Kuroeya, Inc.)

The Contents

The scroll painting shows the street as it was before the Great Bunka Fire of 1806. The 1824 book *Edo kaimono hitori annai* (A guide to shopping on your own in Edo), illustrated by Katsushika Hokusai (1760–1849) with an introduction by Ōta Nanpo (1749–1823), published by the Osaka firm Nakagawa Hōzandō, shows only about a quarter of the eighty-eight shops depicted in *Kidai Shōran*. Clearly the conflagration caused severe damage.

In this scroll painting, the townscape is portrayed in great detail. Gatekeepers, security officers, and shopkeepers are plainly depicted, as are foremen, construction workers, shop caretakers, a fortuneteller, and a seller of malt syrup. Town divisions are distinctly marked by gates and cross streets starting at Imagawabashi Bridge: Honshiroganechō 2-chōme, Honkokuchō 2-chōme (north), Honkokuchō 2-chōme (south), Jikkendana, Honchō 2-chōme (north), Honchō 2-chōme (south), Muromachi 3-chōme, Muromachi 2-chōme, Muromachi 1-chōme.

In all, 1,671 people appear in the scroll, most of them men; there are only 200 women. Small wonder that a pretty woman walking down the street—or a woman in a teahouse—should attract attention. As far as animals go, there are numerous horses, oxen, and especially dogs, the prevalence of the latter bringing to mind the three things Edo was proverbially famous for: "Ise merchants, Inari shrines, and dog excrement." Oxen are shown pulling oxcarts, which were useful in transporting heavy loads up the many slopes and across the many arched bridges in Edo. So-called ox-towns, corresponding to present-day transport depots, were located in Ushigome, Takanawa, and Tenmachō.

What of the shops? At Honkokuchō Jikkendana, we see the sushi shop Tamazushi (pages 17, 23)—the forerunner of today's Nihonbashi establishment—run by Okinaya Shōbei. In Jikkendana, a doll fair is underway (pages 31, 36), thronged with people seeking to buy *hina* dolls and the stands for their display, as well as sprays of peach blossoms for decoration. Nihonbashi Kiya, the famous cutlery specialty shop, was established in 1792. Here we see four Kiya shops in a row (page 52); one, Kiya Koushichi's shop, is under construction, with a construction gang hard at work. A placard on the temporary outer enclosure reads, "Open for business in the warehouse."

The word *muyō* (prohibited), written on a wooden fence by the gate next to a torii mark, stands for *shouben muyō*: "urinating prohibited." Up and down the street are hawkers and peddlers; a used-clothing salesman, wares draped over a wooden pole, peering out from an alleyway; itinerant pilgrims, visitors to Konpira Shrine, and people soliciting for a temple; travelers, elderly couples, and a bachelor moving house; a hairdresser on his way to a customer; the leader of a troupe of actors; and a variety of street performers such as lute-playing priests, shakuhachi-playing Zen monks, and popular religious performers. We see mothers and fathers with their children in tow; a blossom-viewing party; men casting admiring glances at a lovely young woman; for-hire palanquins and scurrying couriers; samurai on their way to and from the castle, each with his spearman, luggage-bearer, sandal-bearer, and other attendants; and samurai bearing congratulatory gifts and betrothal gifts. The final highlight is a brawl in the vicinity of the fish market at Nihonbashi Bridge, so real we can almost hear the yelling.

It takes time to appreciate the depth of *Kidai Shōran* and fully enjoy its 1,671-character pageantry. But this wonderful scroll painting allows us to slip back more than two hundred years in time and see just what daily life was like in old Edo.

Tracing the Scroll's Chinese Roots

IN 2003, KIDAI SHŌRAN TRAVELED TO JAPAN, where it was displayed in its entirety for the first time in a special exhibit entitled "The 808 Towns of Old Edo," held to mark the four-hundredth anniversary of the founding of Edo, and the tenth anniversary of the founding of the Edo-Tokyo Museum. In 2006, the scroll again journeyed to Japan for a special exhibit entitled "Nihonbashi Picture Scroll," held to celebrate the opening of the Mitsui Memorial Museum.

In November, 2009, a replica of the scroll was made on custom-made *washi* paper, 1.4 times the size of the original. It was put on permanent display in the Tokyo Metro Mitsukoshimae Station underground concourse, thanks to the efforts of the Meikyō Nihonbashi Hozon-kai (Society to Preserve the Famous Nihonbashi Bridge) and the Nihonbashi Renaissance 100th Anniversary Planning Committee. The Asian Art Museum of the National Museums in Berlin approved the project, and oversaw the inclusion of commentary from the original edition of this book.

In 2017, in cooperation with Beijing's Capital Museum and Palace Museum, the Edo-Tokyo Museum held a special exhibit entitled "Edo and Beijing: Cities and Urban Life in the 18th Century," in which *Kidai Shōran* was compared to a similar Chinese work of art. In a groundbreaking essay included in the exhibition catalog, Eriguchi Yūko of the Edo-Tokyo Museum indicated that *Kidai Shōran* was influenced by *Wanshou Shengdian* (Grand Ceremony for the Imperial Birthday), an illustrated Chinese text dating from the Qing dynasty. *Kidai* ("prosperous age") is written with an unusual character that was used in the name of Emperor Kangxi (born in 1654; reigned 1662–1722). Based on that similarity, Prof. and Mrs. Hans-Joachim Küster, the collectors of Chinese art who came into possession of *Kidai Shōran*, originally thought that the scroll might be connected to the Chinese emperor. In 2018, the Asian art periodical *Kokka* (vol. 1474) published an explication of the scroll by Kobayashi Tadashi, along with an article by Eriguchi setting out her research on the influence of *Wanshou Shengdian*.

Wanshou Shengdian is a book of woodcut illustrations taken from the 120-volume *Wanshou Shengdian Chuji* (Grand Ceremony for the Imperial Birthday, Premier Compilation; 1716), an account of celebrations held in Beijing in 1713 on the occasion of Emperor Kangxi's sixtieth birthday. It contains prints especially from the main section (vols. 41 and 42). Engraver Zhu Gui (n.d.) made a book based on 148 double-page woodcuts by artists Wang Yuanqi (1642–1715), Song Junye (ca. 1662–1713), and others. The prints are a record of celebrations along the route of the procession of Emperor Kangxi and the empress dowager from the city outskirts to the Forbidden City. Besides *Wanshou Shengdian*, there is also a silk picture scroll in the Palace Museum, a woodblock-print copy of which was recorded in the *Siku quanshu* (Complete Library of the Four Treasuries) in 1780 as *Wanshou Shengdian Chuji*.

Careful comparison of the depiction of eighteenth-century Beijing in *Wanshou Shengdian* and that of early-nineteenth century Edo in *Kidai Shōran* has yielded a valuable hint: it is likely that the artist and/or commissioner of *Kidai Shōran* had access to either the 1713 or 1780 version of the Chinese work. Indeed, figures in the scroll such as a father taking his child to enroll in a *terakoya* school, a street cleaner, and others do have counterparts in *Wanshou Shengdian*. Overall, however, there is a great difference between the rendering of imperial ceremonies and the distinctive Beijing cityscape versus the liveliness of the Nihonbashi street and the daily lives of the people there. Continued research based on this perspective will no doubt lead to more answers.

Kidai Shōran is now widely known in Japan, even appearing in elementary school social studies textbooks. The discovery of its two missing companion scrolls—the *chi* (earth) and *jin* (humankind) volumes—would be warmly welcomed.

THE CITY OF EDO TRACES ITS ROOTS BACK TO 1590, when Tokugawa Ieyasu (1543–1616), who established the Edo government in 1603, ordered the land divided to make towns and streets. With Edo Castle in the center, the lower reaches of the Hirakawa River were diverted to form moats leading away from the castle in a spiral shape. Mount Kanda was leveled to fill in an estuary, forming a townsmen district for merchants and craftsmen.

The townsmen district, modeled after a similar area in Kyoto, was divided into neighborhoods approximately 108 meters square. The developed land on the southern side of Nihonbashi Bridge, which was built in 1603, lies at a 45-degree angle to the land on the northern side, but all the neighborhood segments were neatly aligned. The five highways of the Edo period were laid out with Nihonbashi Bridge as their starting point: Nakasendō, Nikkō Kaidō, and Ōshū Kaidō to the north; Tōkaidō to the south; Kōshū Kaidō to the west.

The *machi* (town districts) shown in *Kidai Shōran*, beginning at the northern side of Nihonbashi Bridge and proceeding straight to Imagawabashi Bridge, run as

follows. First come Muromachi 1-chōme, 2-chōme, and 3-chōme, all three of which straddle both sides of the street. From that point on, however, the numbering system changes to indicate relative proximity to Edo Castle, looming to the west, and the road itself acts as the border dividing the various towns. On the west side of the street comes Honchō 2-chōme, with shops clearly portrayed, while across the street on the east side is Honchō 3-chōme, portrayed only by rooftops. After Honchō comes Jikkendana, followed by Honkokuchō 2-chōme and 3-chōme, then Honshiroganechō 2-chōme and 3-chōme, and finally Imagawabashi Bridge. Honchō Street, intersecting with Nihonbashi Street near the midpoint, was the main thoroughfare leading to the castle. Because of the different layouts of the towns, some east-west and others north-south, gates maintained by each community occur sometimes at corners and sometimes midway between them. The map shows the borders of the towns along Nihonbashi Street.

The map appears slightly distorted because the streets do not intersect at right angles. This is characteristic of land division dating back to the very beginning of the city.

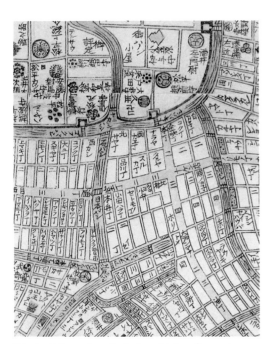

Nihonbashi Street, from *Bunka 2 nen Edo ōezu* (Large plan of Edo, 1805), published by Suharaya Ichibei and Suharaya Zengorō. (Tokyo Metropolitan Foundation for History and Culture Image Archives)

Streets and Districts *in the Vicinity of Nihonbashi*

Kidai Shōran

Hand scroll, ink and colours on paper, 43.7 x 1232.2 cm.
Japan, Tokugawa period.
© Staatliche Museen zu Berlin, Museum für Asiatische
Kunst, former collection of Hans-Joachim and Inge Küster,
gift of Manfred Bohms, 2002-17

The Scroll in its Entirety

Honchō 2-chōme (south)

Honchō Street

Honchō 2-chōme (north)

Jikkendana

Honkokuchō 2-chōme (south)

Honkokuchō Street

Honkokuchō 2-chōme (north)

Honshiroganechō 2-chōme

Honshiroganechō Street

Riverfront

Southern end of the bridge

Imagawabashi Bridge, Kanda

Northern end of the bridge

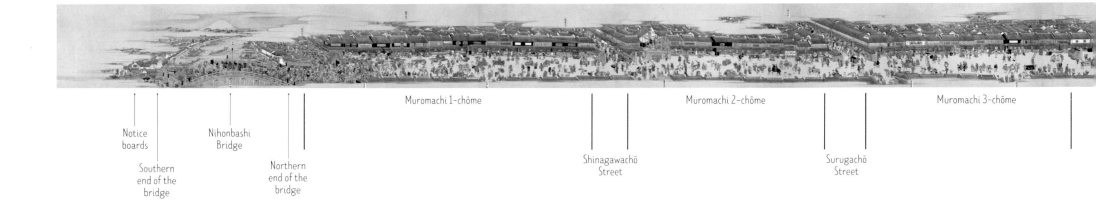

Notice
boards

Southern
end of the
bridge

Nihonbashi
Bridge

Northern
end of the
bridge

Muromachi 1-chōme

Shinagawachō
Street

Muromachi 2-chōme

Surugachō
Street

Muromachi 3-chōme

Strolling through
Kidai Shōran

The time: 1805

The place: Nihonbashi Street, from Imagawabashi Bridge, Kanda, to Nihonbashi Bridge, a total of 760 meters

Energetically and noisily going about their business along the street are 1,671 men, women, and children; twenty dogs; thirteen horses; four head of oxen; one monkey; and two birds of prey. The street is enlivened by hawkers and peddlers, book-lenders, used clothing sellers, hairdressers, worshippers, temple solicitors, pilgrims, mendicant priests, palanquin-bearers, couriers, a flower-viewing party, samurai going to and from the castle, and a doll fair.

This is an "excellent view of a prosperous era in Edo."

Ceramic wholesaler

Ceramic wholesaler

Malt syrup store banner

Malt syrup store (Nagai Koemon)

Ceramic wholesaler

Two-story tenement

Imagawabashi Bridge, Kanda

Teahouse at the foot of the bridge

Ceramic wholesaler (Kameya)

Captions above the scroll identify store names, businesses, signboards, and gates dividing the *machi* or towns. Captions in bold indicate names written in black on gold paper labels affixed to the scroll.

Captions below the scroll identify people and occupations.

Biwa-playing minstrel

Rice porter

Rokujūrokubu pilgrims

For-hire palanquin

Samurai in the castle's service

Pilgrims

Denture and medicine wholesaler (Matsui, Seiyōtan)

Candle wholesaler (Aizu Ōsumiya)

Neighborhood cistern

Unidentified store

Neighborhood cistern

Shiruko and *zōni* store (Fujiya)

Buddhist image store (Yorozuya)

Storehouse (Suharaya Zengorō)

Standing signboard

Shiroganechō Street

Guardhouse

Town gate

Kyoto fabric and heavy cotton wholesaler (Ōsakaya)

Caterer

Joinery

Book wholesaler (Suharaya Zengorō)

Raincoat wholesaler (Yamadaya Heizaemon)

Gatehouse (selling sweets and sundries)

Town gate

Honshiroganechō

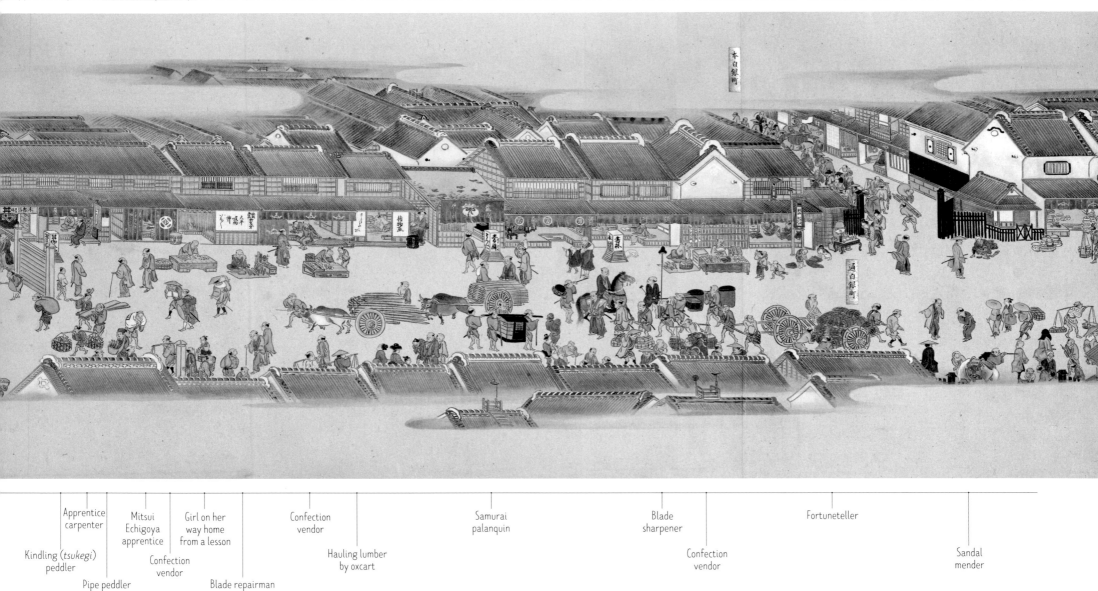

Apprentice carpenter

Mitsui Echigoya apprentice

Girl on her way home from a lesson

Confection vendor

Samurai palanquin

Blade sharpener

Fortuneteller

Kindling (*tsukegi*) peddler

Confection vendor

Hauling lumber by oxcart

Confection vendor

Sandal mender

Pipe peddler

Blade repairman

Mirror workshop
(Tsuda Satsumanojō
Fujiwara Sadaharu)

Tamazushi banner

Ink, brush, and
inkstone wholesaler
(Takashima Yosuke)

Umbrella and *setta*
sandal wholesaler
(Maruya)

Cosmetics store
banner

Water well

Face powder wholesaler
(Sanmojiya)

Sushi shop
(Tamazushi, run by
Okinaya Shōbei)

Neighborhood
cistern

Cosmetics and
accessories
wholesaler
(Tsugane)

Paper
wholesaler?
(Kagaya)

Standing
signboard

Clothing and
fancy goods
wholesaler
(Karakiya)

Seal shop

Tamanoi hair-
oil peddler

Metal-plated
pipe peddler

Returning from sword
practice at the dojo

Mendicant
monks

Physician?

Itinerant performing
monks

Samurai
palanquin

Confection
vendor

Father taking
his son to school,
shouldering a desk

'In this scroll painting, the townscape is portrayed in great detail. Gatekeepers, security officers, and shopkeepers are plainly depicted, as are foremen, construction workers, shop caretakers, a fortuneteller, and a seller of malt syrup. **'** *page 8*

Details enlarged on the following pages

p. 23   p. 22   p. 21   p. 20

通白銀町

御水飴

Fortuneteller
Some things never change. A pair of married women are waiting for information on a straying husband, a ne'er-do-well child, or another of the myriad troubles housewives face. On the table is money wrapped in paper, the fee for having one's fortune told—apparently not a very high one, to judge from the size of the bundles.

Merchant house built in earthen-walled storehouse style
Plaster walls and tiled roofs were initially banned in townhouses as being overly extravagant. However, after the Great Fire of Meireki in 1657 destroyed most of the city, they were encouraged for fire prevention. The foundation of hewn stone, siding of wooden boards, and heavy shutters are other security precautions suitable for a store dealing in high-quality imported ceramic ware. In case of fire, people would climb ladders and nets hung from the wall hooks to pour water on the roof.

"Clean up": *Sōji shiyo*
This fellow, who appears to be sweeping the street, would cry "*Sōji shiyo*" (Clean up!) as he walked along, cleaning the area in front of stores. This hereditary occupation may hark back to medieval times, when people in servitude at shrines and temples performed purification rites. Social conditions in Edo enabled people of all social levels to make a living.

Ceramic wholesale dealer
Alongside large bowls, lipped bowls, and other tableware are items used for hobbies and recreation, such as flower pots and crockery for preparing tea. Gardening was all the rage in the Edo period. Chrysanthemum dolls, gigantic morning glories: such rare and unusual items attracted great attention. Visitors to this store include customers making purchases and hawkers selling their wares as stock.

Father and son on the way to school

"I don't wanna go!" the boy wails, hanging back. Children from ages six to eight began study at *terakoya*, private educational institutions, in February. On the first day, it was customary to bring the writing desk the child would use. (The writer Santō Kyōden used the same desk throughout his life. After he died, his brother Kyōzan donated the desk to Sensōji temple, where it is buried with a memorial stone.) Bento box lunches were popular at this time.

Child pilgrim

The sight of a child on a solo pilgrimage, receiving alms and sleeping in temple halls, was by no means uncommon, though long journeys required a permit. Besides trips for government and commercial business, travel was allowed for religious pilgrimages and for convalescence at hot springs. To finance their trips, travelers would beg along the way, and people often responded warmly. Perhaps this child is on his way to Ise Shrine, a popular destination through the ages.

Gate between two districts

A gate in the middle of the road separates two towns. A door would be inconvenient, so the center is left wide open. In a neighborhood like this one, with many large stores, night travel may have been permissible. Gates in the main street were left with a plain wood finish, while those at alley entrances were painted black. Behind the gate is a shop selling false teeth made from boxwood and soapstone.

Girl on her way home from a lesson

The alleyways were filled with houses where unattached samurai and their wives taught merchants' daughters reading and writing as well as sewing, shamisen, tea ceremony, flower arranging, ballad singing, and other refinements expected of young ladies. At age thirteen or fourteen, the girls would go into service at samurai residences to acquire fine manners. Such accomplishments were highly evaluated at matchmaking time.

Itinerant performing monks

Lay monks would dance as they chanted political satire and religious lampoons set to the tunes of sutras. Even though these were the lowest level of Buddhist monk, disregarding them was considered unlucky, and superstitious merchants always gave them a handout. This helps to explain why there were so many itinerant performers in this part of the city.

Lovely young woman

With her hair in the "lantern side-locks" style, featuring wide wings on either side, a lovely young woman attracts admiring glances as she walks down the street. An ornamental accessory called a *bin-sashi* holds the hair in place. The hairstyle first became popular a few years prior to the scroll's creation. This young woman is accompanied by two salesclerks and two maids, so she must be from a very good family.

Blind masseur entering an alleyway

An acupressure massage is refreshing to the body and spirit. When a shopkeeper felt fatigued, he would send a boy or girl running to fetch the *anma* or masseur. *Anma* were also skilled conversationalists and could entertain their customers with information they had overheard on the job. Being able to come by information, products, and services without stirring from home was a great benefit of city life.

Shop signs

An impressive vertical sign reads, "Seal shop." Seals were important in Edo society, and seal-carvers everywhere did a brisk business. Further down the street is a standing signboard for Tsugane, a wholesale dealer in rouge and fancy goods that reads, "Dealer in combs, hairpins, fancy goods, playthings, and rouge." Maruya, a shop specializing in woven hats and leather-soled sandals, has a hanging sign that reads, "Sandals of various kinds." Large signs placed in the street were effective advertising, but a hindrance to street traffic.

Dog sniffing at vomit
Someone had too much to drink and
threw up in the street. Local *sake* was
cheap, but *sake* from the Kyoto-Osaka
region was fairly expensive. Probably
only gentlemen of the merchant class
could afford to drink enough of it to get
drunk. Drinking contests were popular,
and though the alcohol content of the
sake consumed may have been low, some
stalwart contenders could put away 5 *shō*
(9 liters) or 1 *to* (18 liters).

Party of samurai
Only samurai of a certain rank could visit the
castle on horseback, so this horse, with its
neatly bound mane and fine harness, is the
Edo equivalent of an official limousine. The
rider was always accompanied by a servant
carrying a ladle to give the horse water, as well
as a spearman, a luggage bearer, and a sandal
bearer. The samurai would wear ceremonial
dress to the castle and pack a lunch, a change
of clothes, and other necessities in his luggage.

Rain barrels and weathervanes
Edo was extremely vulnerable to fires.
Both samurai districts and townsmen
districts were required to have fire
lookout towers, and along Nihonbashi
Street with its many large stores, many
rooftops had a rain barrel and a lookout
with a weathervane. When the fire bell
rang, alerting people to a fire somewhere
in the city, someone would climb up to
check the location of the fire and the
direction of the wind.

Famous sushi shop "Tamazushi"
This shop is mentioned in *Edo kaimono
hitori annai*, a shopping guide to the
city published in 1824. (It is said that
the shop moved to Ginza in the Meiji
era [1868–1912].) Tamazushi was the
first sushi shop on Nihonbashi Street,
specializing in catering rather than
serving food on the premises. It started
as a street stand. The auspicious
trademark on the shop curtain is a
sacred ball-shaped gem called a *hōju*.

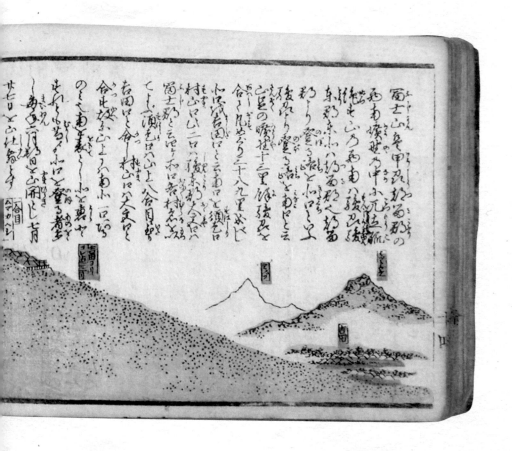

The Luxurious Travels of Lucky Retirees.
See page 29.

Tabikagami (Travel guide).
(Private collection)

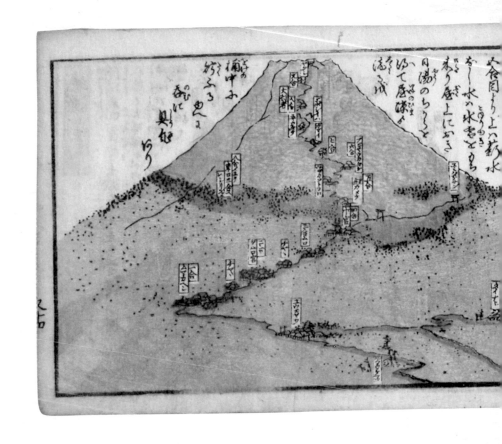

Edo Surugachō nentō no zu (Surugachō in Edo at the first of the year). (Mitsui Bunko)

Ledger chest, Sakata, Yamagata, 19th century, Edo period. (The Japan Folk Crafts Museum)

THE CASTLE TOWNS OF TSU AND MATSUSAKA, located along the road to Ise, were important strategic points between Edo and western Japan. The founder of the Tokugawa shogunate, Tokugawa Ieyasu, attached great importance to them, and chose Tōdō Takatora (1556–1630), daimyō of Iyo-Imabari and a man of political and economic acumen, to be lord of the Tsu domain in Ise province. The area flourished till the mid-eighteenth century, serving as a base for the distribution of goods and information and producing cultural luminaries such as philosopher Motoori Norinaga (1730–1801), an eminent scholar in Shintō and Japanese classics, and botanist Noro Genjō (1693–1761), the shogun's personal physician and a scholar of Western studies. At the same time, the town provided a base for Ise merchants to display their talents.

Commodities from all over could be found in Ise, a junction for land and sea routes. Merchants with a keen sense of fashion and a quick eye for profit excelled at dealing in products from other provinces; after building their financial muscle in Ise, they would set up shop in Kyoto and then, in search of even greater opportunity, head for the huge commercial center of Edo.

Mitsui Takatoshi (1622–1694), founder of the prosperous Mitsui Echigoya store in Edo, was born in Matsusaka. After getting his start in Kyoto, he opened a dry goods store in Edo and achieved great success by introducing over-the-counter trading and a cash-only payment system that accepted no credit. Customers purchased only as much as they needed—from rolls of the finest cloth to mere scraps—and paid on the spot. Instead of the old method of relying on quarterly payments, the store gained an instant influx of cash to use in acquiring stock, creating a flow of supply and demand.

Mitsui employed only trustworthy people from his home province. Anyone who absconded with shop money would be shunned upon his return home, but a steady, honest worker would be looked after for life. Edo stores like his provided a system whereby Ise merchants could recover their capital investment through a community network.

Some enterprises followed the Mitsui Echigoya style of operating in Edo without adapting to Edo business practices; others, like Kiya, established branches on the city outskirts. In the Kiya business model, different branches slightly altered their product lines to avoid competing with each other for customers and to diversify risk.

The majority of merchants throughout Edo were small businessmen who began as street hawkers (*furi-uri*) or "standing vendors" (*tachi-uri*), later acquiring a shop of their own with narrow frontage. Most of the people who visited Nihonbashi Street were such merchants, buying goods from the wholesalers there to stock their own small shops.

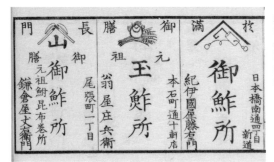

Edo kaimono hitori annai (A guide to shopping on your own in Edo), 1824. (Tokyo Metropolitan Foundation for History and Culture Image Archives)

Edo Merchants' Roots:
Ise Merchants on the Rise

Surugachō Echigoya store signboard, front (top) and back (below). (Isetan Mitsukoshi Ltd.)

THE OWNERS OF THE STORES LINING Nihonbashi Street employed only males from their home provinces to fill positions from apprentices to store managers. It was an age of high infant mortality, so the eldest and next-eldest sons would remain at home to be groomed as heirs; the rest were apprenticed out before the age of ten. In the male-centered merchant houses, even housework was the responsibility of apprentices—from taking personal care of the master to cooking and cleaning. There was a tacit rule that management would turn a blind eye if the youngest apprentices pilfered money for sweets. Labor costs were cheap, so the loss was written off as a necessary expense.

During the six to ten years of an apprenticeship, returning home was generally not allowed. Sometimes, however, after the third year of service, an apprentice judged to have done well in learning the business could return to the home province for a visit. This was also an occasion for them to make their first appearance at the main branch of the store.

After serving out his apprenticeship, an employee would be promoted to shop assistant and then clerk. At this point he would get a nameplate hanging from the ceiling and could finally have clients of his own. He would do business with them in a soft-sounding Kansai dialect that heightened the store's air of sophistication.

Each higher rung attained on the ladder of success, up to the level of head clerk or store manager, brought a corresponding increase in salary. But only a very few ever attained such heights. Many were sent to branch stores once they had attained a certain rank. Others fell by the wayside and returned home. Besides familiarity with social trends, merchants in Edo needed to be inventive in dealing with the city's frequent fires. Large stores damaged by fires might dispose of the unburned merchandise at sales held in the ruins, for example. They would also keep a supply of lumber on hand at all times so that they could rebuild swiftly and get right back in business. Whether a fire caused a business to shrink or expand depended on the manager's quick-wittedness. Having a plan to become a purveyor of goods to the shogunate or to a regional lord was another key to success.

A Merchant's Career Path: A Rocky Road

Interior of Mitsui Echigoya, from *Kinsei shokuninzukushi ekotoba* (Illustrated story of various artisans), by Kuwagata Keisai. (TNM Image Archives)

Career board game *Kotobuki shusse dai sugoroku* (Great board game of lucky advancement). (Tokyo Metropolitan Foundation for History and Culture Image Archives)

"The Apprentice's Holiday," from *Edo funai ehon fūzoku ōrai* (Picture book of Edo genre scenes). (National Diet Library)

THERE WAS NO MANDATORY RETIREMENT AGE in the Edo period. Most business-minded merchants tended to lead abstemious lives until the age of forty or fifty, refraining from drinking, gambling, and buying the favors of women. They would retire after doubling their assets, set up a villa in the suburbs of Mukōjima, and use their hard-earned money to keep a mistress and enjoy a peaceful life. This was held to be the ideal way of spending one's old age.

The Edo metropolis was ideal for achieving this pleasant lifestyle. Food and other necessities of life were sold door-to-door, and special items could be ordered from an "order taker" (goyōkiki). Living space in the city was cramped, and people got along by paring down their possessions, not letting them pile up. Many items that were not daily necessities were available on loan. When cooking was a bother, one could go to a restaurant for a meal made with fresh seasonal foods, or hire a chef, or use a catering service. Bookstores clustered in the city center published books, single-sheet maps and colorful woodblock prints called nishiki-e—thus providing a wealth of information to the townsfolk. Lending libraries were a particularly useful source of intellectual stimulation for retirees.

The elderly of the time were vulnerable to disease, and many suffered from a decline in overall physical strength as well as weakened eyesight, hearing, and teeth. To serve them, the Nihonbashi neighborhood had plenty of pharmacies, as well as denturists who could craft a set of false teeth to order, using boxwood and soapstone.

The diary of one such resident, written in the Kaei era (1848–1855), tells much about life for retirees. Hara Hidejirō, the head of Iwai village in Sodegaura, had come to Edo, where he became factotum to a hatamoto (direct retainer to the shogun). After retiring to his village, however, he found that he missed the pleasures of city life, and soon returned to the city, where he took a house and enjoyed a full and trendy life. His diary indicates that he had a denturist named Matsui make him a set of false teeth; the medicine wholesale dealer and denture-maker Matsui shown in Kidai Shōran is perhaps that one's predecessor. Hara also owned spectacles, bought medicine, and received moxibustion treatment.

In hopes of attaining peace in the next world, it was customary to perform a memorial service prior to one's death that featured the release of one of a variety of caged animals, including loaches, turtles, birds, and monkeys. Hara's diary tells us that he went to Nihonbashi as usual on the first day of the New Year, looking for a fish with which to perform the ceremony. As there were no fish to be had, he returned the next day. It's easy to picture fish from the fish market being released back into the river.

Denkasawa Rokurō no zu (Six old men chat over tea), by Utagawa Kuniyoshi. (National Diet Library)

A Merchant's Life Plan:
The Pleasures of Retirement

Shokusanjin shōzō (Portrait of Shokusanjin), inscription by Ōta Nanpo, picture by Chōbunsai Eishi. (TNM Image Archives)

After years of hard work building up their savings, many retirees would embark on the trip of a lifetime. Visiting shrines and temples provided the pretext, though sightseeing and pleasure-seeking might have been the real goal. When applying to the senior town administrator for permission to travel, declaring the purpose of the trip to be an Ise pilgrimage ensured the quick granting of a permit.

Combining a religious pilgrimage with visits to a number of provinces for sightseeing often meant a trip of one or two months. A retiree from a large store would need capital of two or three hundred *ryō*. He would carry along promissory notes, and when in need of cash would take a tally to a local money-changer of the right affiliation.

The journeys were made on foot as long as the traveler was still able to get around, with servants to carry the luggage. Walking seven or eight hours a day was par. A traveler on the Tōkaidō road would leave from Nihonbashi, be ferried across the Tama River at the Rokugo crossing, and spend his first night at the Kawasaki post town. Those seeing him off would sometimes go as far as Kawasaki and stay overnight with him, making merry to raise the traveler's spirits. The next day, he would go as far as the Odawara post town, and lodge there to prepare for the mountain crossing at Hakone.

Traveling was never without its problems. Rain-swollen rivers could bring a journey to a halt for days on end, and sections of boat travel could be slowed by becalming. A weary traveler could always refresh himself with a visit to nearby hot springs or take his time exploring local culture and sights and getting to know the people. A parcel delivery service was already available, and at every juncture along the way he could buy local specialties and entrust them to an express messenger who would ensure that they arrived at his home in Edo about the same time he did.

Edoites making a pilgrimage to Ise would stop at famous points along the way. After bowing to sacred Mount Fuji from the heights of Hakone, they would proceed to Atsuta Shrine in Nagoya, then the Great Buddha in the old capital of Nara. In Kyoto, they would make the rounds of the shrines and temples and visit the Imperial Palace. Those aspiring to be reborn on Mount Potalaka, the mythical dwelling of the Buddhist bodhisattva Kannon, would follow the mountainous Kumano route to make a circuit of the thirty-three Kansai temples with statues of Kannon.

After crossing to Shikoku Island to worship at Konpira Shrine, travelers would cross back to visit Itsukushima Shrine on the island of Miyajima. If they managed to squeeze in a trip north to Miyazu Bay on the Tango Peninsula, they would have seen three of the country's most famous views: Mount Fuji, Itsukushima Shrine, and Amanohashidate, the scenic sand bar spanning the bay.

This marked the most distant point of the sightseeing trip from Edo. All that remained was to stop by Zenkōji temple in Nagano before heading for home. Having successfully completed his grand tour, the retiree could regale his family and friends with stories of his journey.

Ise pilgrimage depicted in *Ise sangū Miyagawa no watashi* (Crossing the Miyagawa river to visit Ise Shrine), by Utagawa Hiroshige.
(Kanagawa Prefectural Museum of Cultural History)

Merchants on the Road:
The Luxurious Travels of Lucky Retirees

Kane no waraji (Golden sandals) vol. 1, written and illustrated by Jippensha Ikku.
(Inagaki Shin'ichi)

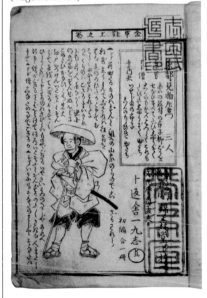

Vacant store? | Medicine wholesaler (Hodōen) | Neighborhood cistern | Umbrella and sandal wholesaler (Iseya) | Decorative-paper wholesaler (Maruya Hikobei) | Standing signboard | Neighborhood cistern | Storehouse (Maruya Hikobei) | Storehouse (Imasu, Kazusaya) | Entrance to Honshiroganechō 2-chōme | Silk and cotton wholesaler (Imasu, Kazusaya) | Stole and robe wholesaler (Izumiya) | Gatehouse (sweets and sundries store) | Kokuchō Street | Town gate | Neighborhood cistern | Guardhouse | Tobacco wholesaler (Ōtaya)

Strolling through Kidai Shōran PART II

From Honkokuchō to Jikkendana and Honchō

For-hire palanquin | Shakuhachi-playing monks | Masseur | Couriers | Street-stall teahouse | Money-lending monk | Hair-oil and hair-tying-cord peddler | Bamboo peddler | Board peddler | Green vegetable peddler | Shakuhachi-playing monks | Tobi vigilantes | Fishmonger | Sake delivery boy

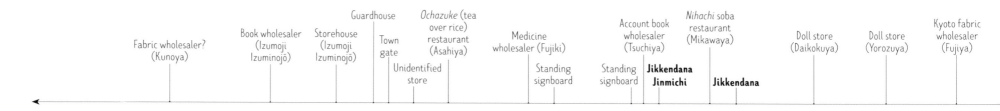

Fabric wholesaler?
(Kunoya)

Book wholesaler
(Izumoji
Izuminojō)

Storehouse
(Izumoji
Izuminojō)

Guardhouse

Town
gate

Unidentified
store

Ochazuke (tea
over rice)
restaurant
(Asahiya)

Medicine
wholesaler (Fujiki)

Standing
signboard

Standing
signboard

Account book
wholesaler
(Tsuchiya)

**Jikkendana
Jinmichi**

Nihachi soba
restaurant
(Mikawaya)

Jikkendana

Doll store
(Daikokuya)

Doll store
(Yorozuya)

Kyoto fabric
wholesaler
(Fujiya)

Single woman
moving house

Procession
bearing
betrothal gifts

Doll store

Doll store

Samurai
palanquin

Jikkendana doll
fair

Buddhist altar equipment wholesaler (Nishimura, Yorozuya Ichibei)

Pipe wholesaler (Nakamuraya Genpachi)

Dry goods, bag, and pouch wholesaler (Marugakuya)

Entrance to Honchō 2-chōme

Storehouse (Tamaya)

Rouge, powder, and aloeswood-oil wholesaler (Tamaya)

Cosmetics wholesaler signboard

Cosmetics wholesaler banner

Gatehouse (sweets and sundries store)

Honchō Street

Town gate

Guardhouse

Tavern

Entrance to Honchō 3-chōme

Medicine wholesaler (Konishi Rinbei)

Standing signboard

Dry goods and face powder wholesaler (Oumiya)

Monkey trainer

Bird catcher

Street stand selling sushi?

Pipe vendor

Confection stand (Kiriya)

Hauling stone blocks by oxcart

Blossom-viewing party carrying a picnic lunch

Pilgrims

Water vendor

Street-stall teahouse

News-sheet vendors

Soliciting donations for temple construction

Rice polisher

Details enlarged on the following pages

p. 38   p. 37   p. 36   p. 35   p. 34

通石町

Musclemen: Bamboo-seller and board-seller

Carefully maintaining his balance, the bamboo-pole seller walks along with a heavy load of green bamboo. Under the pole across his shoulders he carries a smaller pole as a lever, which cleverly allows him to support the load at three places. Even Edoites of small build managed to carry around merchandise weighing nearly 50 kilograms, much to their credit. Bamboo was primarily a building material, but it was also widely used for laundry poles and other things.

"Vegetables, green vegetables!"

Hawkers sell fresh produce they've bought at the morning market. Burdock, sweet potatoes, and long onions were widely sold from Nihonbashi to Yushima. These, and other vegetables such as *daikon* radishes, were raised by farmers using the night soil collected from Edo residents as fertilizer. This was Edo-style recycling.

Parent and child, hand in hand

High infant mortality made children extra precious. An infant was christened on the seventh day after birth and taken to the local shrine on the thirtieth day. At each stage, the parents rejoiced and prayed for their child's continued health. To ensure there would be an heir to the family business, a man might sire children with his mistress as well as his wife—or he might bring a talented individual into the family through adoption.

Tobi: Checkpoint guards, firemen, scaffolding men

The *tobi* were vigilantes who served as firemen and as guards at checkpoints. These *tobi* are wearing matching *momohiki* work pants and carrying pewter staffs that jingle when they shake them on patrol. If a brawl were to break out, they would be the ones to rush over to restore peace. Sons of Edo were known for their hot tempers, though, and sometimes they, too, could be found in the thick of a ruckus. Their day job was manning the scaffolding at construction sites.

A graceful pair of *komusō* priests

The men wearing black lacquered geta clogs and deep basket hats hiding their faces are *komusō*, Zen monks of the Fuke sect. These monks played the shakuhachi flute as a form of meditation and as a means of collecting alms. These two have a lissome air, reminiscent of figures in ukiyo-e prints by Kitagawa Utamaro (1753–1806), whose life was nearing its end around the time this scroll was painted. The Edo world portrayed here is one that Utamaro knew intimately.

Maruya, a paper wholesaler

Edo people were huge consumers of paper. Reams of it were needed for account books and ledgers, and foreign visitors were amazed by the sight of people using it to blow their noses. Maruya dealt in every kind of paper; *karakami*, the type advertised here, was a sturdy variety originally introduced from China. Edo became a sophisticated information society thanks to a stable supply of paper from a number of production areas.

The moneylender

There is something suspicious about this man's bamboo hat and staff, for he is a moneylender—or, more plainly, a loan shark. Shady monks might collect money on the pretext of building a temple and parlay that into funds to lend out at high interest. A passing samurai points an accusing finger as if to say, "Take advantage of people's weakness, and you'll suffer divine retribution!"

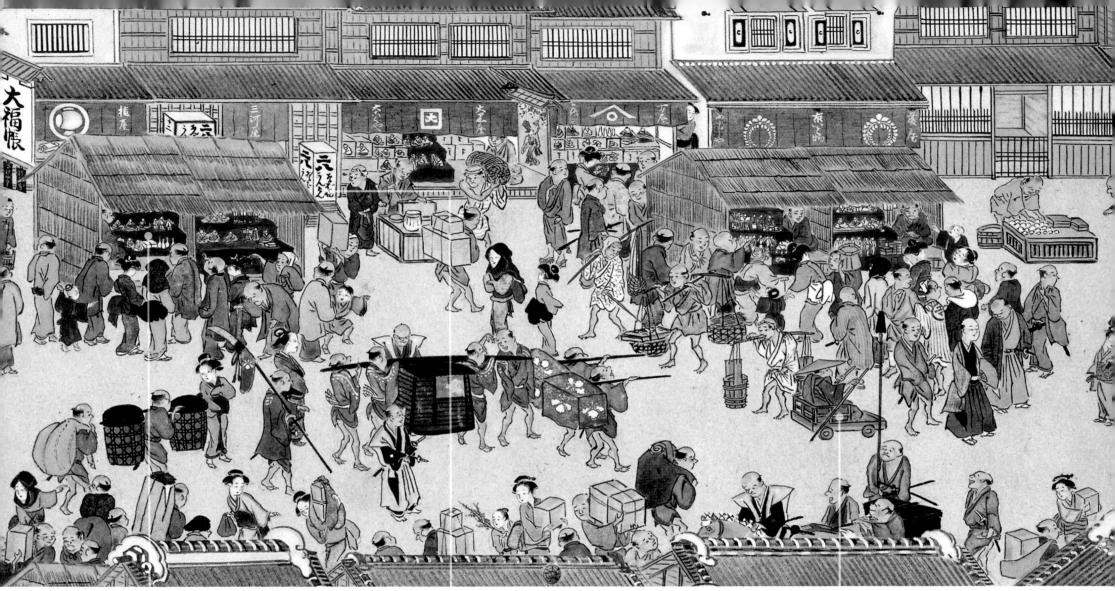

A springtime tradition: The Jikkendana Doll Fair

Jikkendana (ten stores) got its name because it began as ten makeshift stores. The Doll Festival celebrated on March 3 originated in an ancient purification ritual in which dolls meant to bear human impurities were placed in the river to float away. In the Edo period, it became customary to celebrate the day at home with tiered displays, including a pair of emperor and empress dolls and their attendants. Prices at the doll fair were negotiable, leading to spirited haggling.

Mikawaya noodle shop

This soba (buckwheat noodle) shop is poised to serve hungry shoppers and sightseers. It started out as a street stand serving *nihachi* ("two eight") noodles (so called because they sold for 16 [2 x 8] *mon*, equivalent to ¥480 or around US$4.50 in today's prices).

A beriberi sufferer

The man in a wheelchair is likely suffering from beriberi, known as the "Edo sickness." Edoites took pride in eating highly refined and polished white rice, but as a result some suffered from vitamin B1 deficiency. While rural areas of Japan often experienced famine, the capital was awash in rice, because Edo samurai traded in their rice stipends for cash.

A taxi-horse

The maximum load for a horse was 180 kilograms, the weight of three bales of rice. If the load was light enough, a person could ride along on this "Edo taxi." Judging by her direction, this lovely traveler may have ridden here from the post town of Senju.

A single woman moving house

Fires were common in Edo, and those who lost their homes had to find new lodgings. It was common to see people pack up their few belongings and move. A woman who lived in the narrow confines of a row house had scant household goods, as seen here. But the ability to move freely as one's status changed was another perk of urban life.

Handsome florists

Florists were reputed to be good-looking men; many a drama featured the prodigal son of a distinguished family taking on the guise of a flower-seller. A gentle spirit presides over spring flowers. Sprigs of peach blossoms are stylishly arranged, ready for display on Doll Festival tiers. The sight of flowers being bought and sold was unique to cities.

Enjoying a midday drink

A restaurant with an attractive round window advertises its *chazuke*, a simple meal of hot tea on boiled rice, but it also welcomed well-off townsmen or samurai who had time for a convivial midday drink. Customers no doubt enjoyed having a pretty young waitress fill their *sake* cups. A scene of peace and tranquility.

Oxen in Edo

In Edo, horse riding was for members of the samurai class. Heavy loads were pulled by oxen or men. In Kyoto, the aristocracy rode in ox-drawn carriages, but in Edo, oxen were used for physical labor and convenient, if slow, door-to-door deliveries. Shibakurumachō in Takanawa, Edobashi-hirokoji and Hachōbori all had ox towns, the equivalent of today's freight depots.

Samurai women on an outing

A party of samurai women are on a flower-viewing expedition; a servant carrying lunch and a two-handled keg follows them. They appear excited and light of heart, and are headed, perhaps, for the hills of Ueno or the banks of the Sumida River. The sight of women out by themselves enjoying the seasonal attractions, going to the theater, boating, or visiting shrines and temples surprised foreign missionaries when they arrived in the late sixteenth century.

Newspaper vendors reading aloud the latest news

Two men wear deep straw headgear to hide their faces as they promote an illicit news sheet, ready to flee the moment a policeman shows up. One stands guard while the other artfully reads aloud anything from criticism of the authorities to news of a double suicide, a revenge tale, or palace incidents. To find out more, townsfolk must buy a copy. These early newspapers/gossip rags were printed using woodblocks.

Soliciting for the erection of a temple hall

One of Edo's famous old temples has burned down. To help with its restoration, several old women walk about town together, calling for donations and chanting the Nembutsu devotional formula as they go. Such activities were a sort of old people's club, combining piety, pleasure, and profitability. Getting to see the sights of the city was an added attraction.

**Tamaya, a shop popular
with city girls**
The Edo branch of a leading
cosmetics shop based in Kyoto.
At the time this scroll was painted,
a perfume called "Kumoi-kō,"
advertised on the big sign out
front, was extremely popular.
The containers for Kyoto cosmetics
in this exclusive shop look lovely.

Gatehouse: an Edo-style convenience store
The gatehouse is a small, jerry-built structure next
to the gate. The gateman's main duties were to close
the gate at night and open it in the morning, to care
for abandoned children, and to watch for fire and
thieves. At first, only single men could take the job,
but later gatemen were allowed to marry and have
a family. The salary was low, so to supplement their
income they would sell sweets and sundries—an Edo
version of today's convenience store.

'Edo medicinal culture was rich. *Besides Chinese herbal medicines, there were medicines that had been introduced by foreign traders and missionaries.* page 43 **'**

**Treating Disease:
Supplements, Massage,
Hot Springs**
See page 43

Inshoku yōjō kagami
(Guide to digestive
health), 1850, *nishiki-e*
(colored woodblock print)
by Utagawa Yoshitsuna.
(Tokyo Metropolitan
Foundation for History and
Culture Image Archives)

"Fires and fights are the flowers of Edo," went a popular saying of the time. In the townsmen's districts such as Nihonbashi, row houses made of wood and paper were packed together and the population density was high. When fires broke out in residential areas surrounded by canals, there was no escape but across bridges, thus increasing the damage. The large stores on the main streets had tiled roofs and storehouses, and they carefully followed fire-prevention procedures, but their wood construction meant they were at high risk of fire from flying sparks.

Owners of large stores and other wealthy people stored precious objects in cellars and clay-walled storehouses, and would plaster the joints of the walls when fire broke out to avoid damage. Another way they tried to minimize their losses was to send all but the necessary operating funds back to the main branch in the home province.

Astute shop owners would build a storehouse in the neighborhoods of Honjo or Fukagawa, east of the Sumida River, to spread out their family possessions and merchandise. They also stored enough lumber at a lumberyard to rebuild immediately after a fire. Stores had rooftop fire lookouts with a weathervane attached, and kept a bucket of water handy along with the "seven firefighting tools."

In 1657, the Great Fire of Meireki destroyed the keep of Edo Castle and two-thirds of the city, killing more than 100,000 people. (It was also known as the Furisode or "swaying-sleeved kimono" Fire, said to have been started when a temple priest attempted to burn a cursed kimono.) A second great fire, the Great Meiwa Fire, killed an estimated 15,000 in 1772.

The Nihonbashi of 1805 shown in *Kidai Shōran* burned down on March 4, 1806, in the Great Bunka Fire, the last of the three great Edo-period fire disasters. The fire started at noon and spread north from Shibakurumachō in front of Takanawa Sengakuji temple, engulfing the Moritaza theater near Kyōbashi. Nihonbashi burned to the ground, and the flames reached as far as Kanda and Asakusa, destroying over 530 residential quarters and claiming over 1,200 lives. The greatest damage was done in *shitamachi* where artisans and merchants lived.

Other, smaller fires also caused serious damage. On November 13 of that same year, a fire broke out in the residence of the kabuki wig maker Tomokurō in Nihonbashi and spread to other areas. Tomokurō's own house was protected by a clay-walled storehouse and cellar, and so suffered little damage. Enraged victims of the fire then attacked the wigmaker's house and tore it down, according to *"Waga koromo"* (My clothing), an essay by the physician and writer Katō Eibian (1763–?).

The fear of fires was constant in Edo, and Edoites racked their brains to find ways to fight them. Their quickness in the recovery after a conflagration was also notable.

Chinka anshin zukan (Reassuring almanac of fire control), 1854. Detail right. (National Diet Library)

Edo Merchants and Fires:
Disaster as a Business Opportunity

Traditional Asian medicine was used to maintain and restore health in the Edo period. The study of medicinal plants, minerals, and animal tissues such as rhino horn was a common pastime. Moxibustion and massage were popular forms of treatment for specific points on the body. The shogun Tokugawa Ieyasu even made his own herbal medicines using a druggist's mortar.

One of the policies of Tokugawa Yoshimune (1684–1751), the eighth shogun of the Tokugawa shogunate, was to encourage provincial industries. This saw the increased cultivation of plants used in dyeing, such as *beni* (safflower) in the Akita domain and *ai* (indigo) in the Tokushima domain. It also stimulated the development of herbal medicines, which likewise used many plants. *Hon-beni*, a pigment made from safflower, for example, was used not only for dyeing but was also stored in medicine boxes as a disinfectant.

Edo medicinal culture was rich. Besides Chinese herbal medicines and homegrown prophylactics, there were *nanban* ("southern barbarian") medicines that had been introduced by foreign traders and missionaries in the sixteenth century, as well as imported Dutch medicines from the trading post on the island of Dejima. The medicine wholesalers of Nihonbashi offered all sorts of medications as well as distillation apparatus, scalpels, microscopes, flasks, magnifying glasses, and other instruments used in the Dutch school of medicine.

The most feared sicknesses were smallpox, measles, dysentery, influenza, rubella, cholera, and other contagious diseases for which there were no specific remedies. Edo was a clean city with a good water supply and a sewage system, but the modern concept of public hygiene had not yet taken hold. A storm or flood, for instance, would be followed by an outbreak of dysentery or plague.

Pulmonary tuberculosis was another common fatal disease. Edoites also suffered from so-called luxury diseases such as beriberi, gout, and depression. Women's physiology was not well understood: menopausal symptoms were diagnosed as *nobose* (a rush of blood to the head) and treated as a menstrual disorder. Bleeding to death during childbirth was all too common. Female pain possibly related to gallstones or menstrual cramps was referred to as *shaku* (spasms).

"Sickness starts with the mind," went the saying, and sometimes a psychological shock would lead to blindness or some other ailment. In that case, the sufferer would rely on a shaman for treatment, or put their trust in an amulet.

As travel increased in popularity, people also began seeking treatment from the mineral waters at hot springs. At the same time, the flourishing Edo sex industry in the Yoshiwara pleasure quarters and elsewhere led to a surge in gonorrhea and syphilis, venereal diseases that first entered Japan through contacts with foreigners in the sixteenth century.

Medicine peddler's chest. (Tokyo Metropolitan Foundation for History and Culture Image Archives)

Treating Disease: Supplements, Massage, Hot Springs

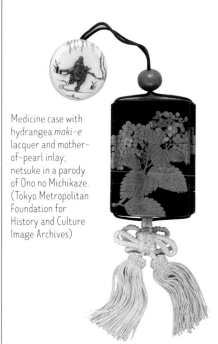

Medicine case with hydrangea *maki-e* lacquer and mother-of-pearl inlay; netsuke in a parody of Ono no Michikaze. (Tokyo Metropolitan Foundation for History and Culture Image Archives)

Fabric
wholesaler
(Yorozuya)

Medicine
wholesaler
(Echigoya)

Account
book
wholesaler
(Osakaya)

Standing
signboard

Medicine,
face powder,
and helmet
wholesaler
(Kagiya)

Medicine
wholesaler
(Fukushimaya)

Standing
signboard

Medicine
and pipe
wholesalers
(Daikokuya
Kichiemon)

Aguramise
(should be
Ukiyo Shōji,
"Floating World
Lane")

Buddhist altar
equipment
wholesaler
(Yorozuya
Ichitarō)

Medicine
wholesaler
(Tawaraya,
Morinoshi)

Medicine
wholesaler
(Yorozuya)

Umbrella
wholesaler
(Nimonjiya)

Standing
signboard

Town gate,
guardhouse

Strolling through
Kidai Shōran
PART III

**From Muromachi
3-chōme to 2-chōme**

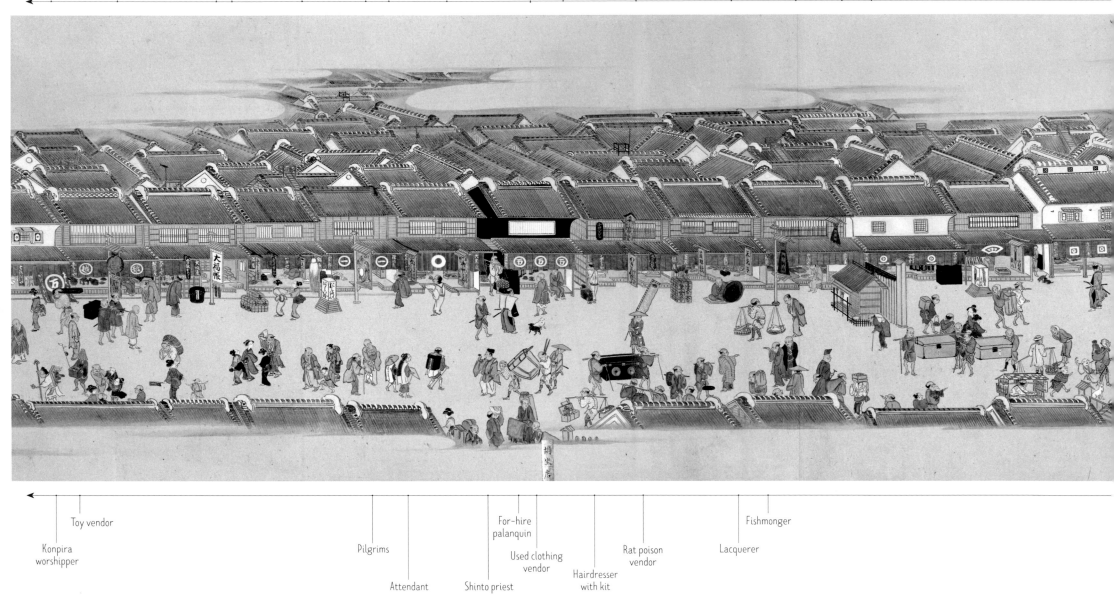

Konpira
worshipper

Toy vendor

Pilgrims

Attendant

Shinto priest

For-hire
palanquin

Used clothing
vendor

Hairdresser
with kit

Rat poison
vendor

Lacquerer

Fishmonger

Small tool
wholesaler

Small tool
wholesaler
(Nagashimaya)

Book
wholesaler
(Suharaya
Ichibei)

Neighborhood
cistern

Surugachō

Textile
painter

Ink, brush, and
inkstone wholesaler
(Nakamuraya
Chūbei)

Standing
signboard

City water
well

Kyoto fabric
and surplice
wholesaler
(Mitsui Echigoya)

Guardhouse

Town
gate

Gatehouse
(sweets and
sundries store)

Town
gate

Cistern
for Mitsui
Echigoya

Dry goods
store (Mitsui
Echigoya)

Standing
signboard

Abacus
wholesaler
(Sashimaya)

Standing
signboard

**Entrance to
Setomonochō**

Pilgrims

Soliciting donations for the
rebuilding of Ekō-in temple
(The donation box is marked
"Bunka 2" [1805])

Guardhouse

Hoop vendor

Toy vendor

Men carrying a
cooking stove

Mitsui Echigoya
delivery boys

Green
vegetable
peddler

Food
deliveryman

Used clothing
vendor

‹ **45**

Fish cake
store

Guardhouse

Town gate

Gatehouse
(sundries store)

Grocery store
(Yaoya)

Store under
construction (Kiya
Koushichi)

**Entrance to
Oda[wara]chō**

Abacus and
small tool
wholesaler
(Kiya)

Small tool
wholesaler
(Kiya)

Small tool
wholesaler
(Kiya)

Small tool
wholesaler
(Kawachiya)

Neighborhood
cistern

Food stall

Kokubu tobacco
vendor

Daikagura circus
performers
(Maruichi)

For-hire
palanquin

Monk and page

For-hire
palanquin

Hoop vendor

Falconers

Bamboo ware
vendor

Elderly couple
moving house

Details enlarged on the following pages

p. 52   p. 51   p. 50   p. 49   p. 48

Hairdresser

Barbershops were places for lively repartee, as depicted in the 1813 comic novel *Ukiyodoko* (Floating world barbershop) by Shikitei Sanba (1776–1822), but wealthy merchants would have hairdressers call at their home. This fine fellow with the red toolbox is like Shinza the Barber in the kabuki play by Kawatake Mokuami (1816–1893). Except for courtesans, women either did their own hair or had a servant do it. Women hairdressers came into vogue around this time, but were banned in the mid-1800s.

Rat poison

The young man is carrying a sign advertising "Iwami Gold Mine Rat Poison," made using arsenious anhydride from the Iwami silver mine. Dogs were ubiquitous in Edo, but rice warehouses also kept cats to stop rodents from nibbling on precious rice stores. The lack of felines appearing in *Kidai Shōran* suggests they were too valuable to allow outdoors.

Raincoat store

The hanging sign is in the shape of an open *kappa*, or raincoat. Made of *washi* paper impregnated with tung oil, the coats were lightweight and waterproof as well as easy to fold. Tung oil, made by pressing the nuts of the tung tree, was easier to obtain than persimmon tannin, which was also waterproof. Samurai always took a *kappa* along with a change of clothes when traveling or visiting the castle.

First fruits of the season

Hatsumono—the very first produce of the season—was in great demand in Edo. The first catch of bonito was especially sought after and brought extremely high prices. In 1686 the shogunate issued an injunction against selling *hatsumono* at high prices, to little effect.

Delivering betrothal gifts
Messengers from a samurai family head for the home of a bride-to-be bearing betrothal gifts. Under the cloth imprinted with the groom's family crest are valuables and an array of symbolic gifts such as sea bream, *noshiawabi* (long, thin strips of dried abalone wrapped in folded red-and-white paper), konbu seaweed, and dried squid.

Konpira pilgrim
On the pilgrim's back is a mask of a *tengu*, a folk figure symbolic of the divinity regarded as the protector of sailors. A similar mask appears in the print of the twelfth stage of Hiroshige's *Fifty-Three Stages of the Tōkaidō* (1833–1834). The mask served a double purpose, enabling pilgrims to advertise their faith and also to solicit alms from those unable to make the pilgrimage. Street performances of prayers and incantations were another way to raise money.

Black water pail
A water pail painted with astringent persimmon is placed here for use in case of fire. Besides helping to preserve wood, persimmon tannin was known to be expensive, which helped advertise the shop's prosperity. Ordinarily, water used in firefighting was kept in dipping buckets placed on city water wells.

Well-to-do family fond of dining out
Edo gourmets frequented fine restaurants such as Yaozen and Hirasei, sparing no expense in indulging their taste for fine food. Drinking wine from a glass cup was commonplace. Edo restaurants serving *shippoku* cuisine, a Nagasaki specialty combining elements of European, Japanese, and Chinese cuisines, were a fad at the time.

Elegant customers

The frontage on the main street was narrow, but Echigoya's shop fronts extended half a block down both sides of Surugachō Street, offering all manner of kimono cloth in bolts and pieces. A kimono in the latest fashion would be ready for pickup about four hours after being ordered. The payment policy was strict: "Cash only, prices as advertised."

Mitsui Echigoya, a wealthy merchant

Edo's largest store is shown with copper rain gutters and red latticed walls. The rain barrel out front, topped by a heap of buckets, speaks of the store's enormous scale and importance. On the right side of Surugachō Street are sellers of kimonos and clothing; on the left are wholesalers dealing in Kyoto fabrics and Buddhist priests' stoles. Echigoya also handled money-changing, using capital gained through cash settlements, and was also the official supplier to the shogunate.

Out-of-town visitors

A pair of visitors in classic travel garb: gaiters and short coat, a walking stick, and a woven hat. One of them is pointing down Edo's busiest street, Surugachō, toward Edo Castle and Mount Fuji. This was the number one sightseeing spot in Edo, the place where, it was said, "Every day a thousand—no, ten thousand—*ryō* change hands." Across the street is Echigoya, the celebrated clothing store of the Mitsui family.

Falconers

The shogun's falconers make an appearance—not an unusual sight, since the castle is not far away. Taking falcons out into a packed street at midday is part of the birds' training, to accustom them to crowds.

Old couple moving house

Piled on the large, two-wheeled, hand-drawn cart are a bucket, an urn, a lampstand with a paper frame, and other household possessions. The lampstand offers a glimpse of the luxurious life the couple once led. Perhaps their shop has folded, bringing hard times and forcing them to move. There is something moving in their plight, suggesting life's fragility. Still, there is dignity in the old woman's face.

A strangely conspicuous couple

The husband is carrying their paper umbrellas, and the wife's obi dangles smartly in the back in what may be the latest fashion. They are probably from the countryside, and passers-by eye them curiously. She: "So *this* is the famous Nihonbashi I've heard so much about! After this, I'm off to buy some choice rouge at Tamaya." He: "I can see this is going to cost me."

The bookstore Suharaya Ichibei

This bookmaker rose to fame in 1774 with the bestselling *Kaitai shinsho* (New book of anatomy), translated from the Dutch. Two other branches were also located on Nihonbashi Street. Big projects were jointly published by stores in Edo, Kyoto, and Osaka, which shared profits and sought to expand their sales networks.

Under construction

Kiya of Nihonbashi lets customers know they are still welcome. "During construction, we're open for business in the storehouse," reads the placard. The hand-drawn two-wheeled cart is loaded with the hewn stones for the foundation. The *tobi* look dashing in traditional work garb—apron-like vests worn over bare chests, tight-fitting *momohiki* drawers—and they intone a workmen's chant as they prepare the framing.

Four Kiya shops in a row

The shop on the right, with the logo showing the character 木 (*ki*, "wood") inside crossed parallel lines, is the forerunner of today's Kiya cutlery shop in Tokyo. Edo Kiya originated when a medicine merchant from Osaka expanded his market to Edo. Each new branch of the same shop had its own specialty, from small tools to flints to soldiers' hats. The shop on the far left is under construction.

Kōmei bijin rokkasen Naniwaya Okita (Renowned beauties likened to the six immortal poets: The waitress Okita of the teahouse Naniwaya), c. 1798, by Kitagawa Utamaro. (TNM Image Archives)

DURING THE EDO PERIOD, TOWNSMEN WERE required to dress in cotton. Most of those living in row houses would have one nice cotton kimono; the ones who could afford more bought them used. Those who were well off, however, began to wear silk garments. The wife and daughters of a wealthy merchant at a large store, for example, would have chests filled with made-to-order kimono, and would dress with striking elegance for events such as sightseeing excursions or trips to the theater. Such opulent displays often brought reproof from the shogunate.

Kidai Shōran depicts Edo culture at its height, and the people seen out and about are colorfully attired. While the men are generally dressed in dark blue or brown, the women are arrayed in pretty shades of red, pink, and saffron. Their obi, too, are lavish. This, of course, was before the Tenpō Reforms of 1841–1843 outlawed ostentatious displays.

Wealthy townsmen took advantage of the laws to refine their sense of style. Fine patterns that were made by adding colorful threads to the weave became chic, along with *komon* material, which was dyed using incredibly intricate stencils in repetitive patterns. Both on first glance appeared plain, but were astonishingly detailed. Another technique was to wear a muted outer garment with a lavish lining and undergarment. Understated hues such as *shibucha*, "astringent brown," and *nezucha*, "gray brown," came into vogue, along with the austere colors favored by actors. Neutral colors took on different tones when paired with other colors. Such subtlety that hid the labor and extravagance of the craftsmanship was considered more luxurious than outright showiness.

Men with financial clout such as wealthy merchants, rice brokers, direct retainers of the shogun, and senior vassals became known as *tsūjin* ("connoisseurs") or *suijin* ("men of refined tastes"). They supported this culture, and saw the latest fads spread from their salons throughout society. Even places of ill repute such as kabuki playhouses and the Yoshiwara red-light district gave rise to cutting-edge fashions that were disseminated through woodblock prints and illustrated fiction.

Edoites were curious and alert to the latest fashion trends. If people heard admiring comments about, say, the style of a certain woman's apron at a popular teahouse across from the Sensōji temple, many would flock there to see for themselves and promptly copy her style. Hairstyles like the topknot for men and the "lantern sidelocks" for women became popular in the same way.

Merchants' Attire:
A Refined Style, Unseen

"Hakoiri musume" (Sheltered girl) from *Edo fūzoku zukan* (Almanac of Edo scenery). (Hosomi Museum)

"Tsūjin" (Connoisseur) from *Edo fūzoku zukan* (Almanac of Edo scenery). (Hosomi Museum)

By the early nineteenth century, the Tokugawa feudal system had been in place for two centuries, and the system of social classes was well established. As long as samurai and townsmen each played their roles, then—barring some natural disaster—everything went smoothly. Life in the city was convenient, with products and information readily available, and everyone could enjoy a degree of luxury in keeping with their status.

Townsmen with resources gave considerable thought to their leisure time, and there was a flourishing culture of various pastimes and amusements. Horticulture was popular, with a preference for plants, especially potted ones, that could be raised in narrow spaces. The cultivation of morning glories soared in popularity in the first half of the nineteenth century. Japanese missions to Tang China had brought the morning glory to Japan in the Nara period (710–794) as a medicinal plant, but in the Edo period it began to be appreciated as an ornamental plant. Different varieties of morning glory were crossbred to produce prized versions. Gardeners vied to come up with interesting variations in the color and shape of the flowers, the speckling of the leaves, and the twist of the stem. Hundreds of new varieties of blue flags, azaleas, *fukujusō* (*Adonis amurensis*), and other flowers attracted throngs at exhibitions.

For the shogun and daimyō, the ultimate pastime became creating gardens with artificial hills, ponds, and flowing water, just as the Heian aristocracy had done. The beauty of nature represented by such gardens was also found in microcosm in the art of bonsai. In this way, everyone from samurai and wealthy merchants to retirees living in row houses with a plot of only 71 square feet could compete in expressing their worldview through gardening.

Enthusiasts would buy a sapling at one of the plant fairs on Ueno Street or elsewhere and spend the next ten or twenty years perfecting its shape. Prosperous townsmen had ceramic pots for their bonsai fired to order, or used pots imported from China. Reflecting this trend, *Kidai Shōran* shows many such flowerpots lined up in front of the ceramics wholesaler near Imagawabashi Bridge.

In the eighteenth century, there was also a vogue for recreating scenic places from around the country through *bonseki*, the art of using stones and sand to create miniature scenes of nature on a tray. Small stones would be arranged on a lacquer tray and surrounded by white sand to represent streams or waves. Such miniature landscaping was immensely popular.

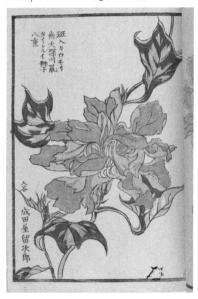

Henge asagao (Mutated morning glory), by Ryōchishū. (Tokyo Metropolitan Foundation for History and Culture Image Archives)

Miniature landscapes in *Kurokamiyama engi emaki* (Illustrated handscrolls of the origins of Kurokamiyama), 1814, text by Nakamura Butsuan, paintings by Kuwagata Keisai. (Kan'eiji)

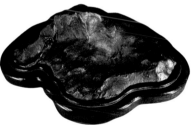

Bonseki (natural stone) "Kurokamiyama." Obtained by Nakamura Butsuan (1751–1834), an Edo Castle master tatami maker, while in Nikkō on the shogun's bidding, recreating a miniature landscape of Kegon Waterfall by Lake Chuzenji, Mount Kurokami, and Mount Futara. (Kan'eiji)

Small tool
wholesaler
(Iseya)

Neighborhood
cistern

Paper
wholesaler
(Echizen'ya)

Grocery and
dry food store
(Yaoya)

Neighborhood
cistern

Miso
wholesaler
(Ōtaya)

Neighborhood
cistern

Lacquerware
wholesaler?
(Iseya)

**Ukiyo Shōji ("Floating World
Lane") Actually Takasago jinmichi;
maybe a misplaced label.**

Confectioner
(Hitachiya)

Small tool
wholesaler
(Iseya)

Neighborhood
cistern

Small tool
wholesaler
(Takashimaya)

Small tool
wholesaler
(Matsudaya)

Medicine (and
lacquerware?) store
(Nishimuraya)

Store selling sandals and
umbrellas (Shimaya)

**Entrance to
Shinagawachō**

Neighborhood
cistern

**Strolling through
Kidai Shōran
PART IV**

**From Muromachi 1-chōme to
Nihonbashi Bridge**

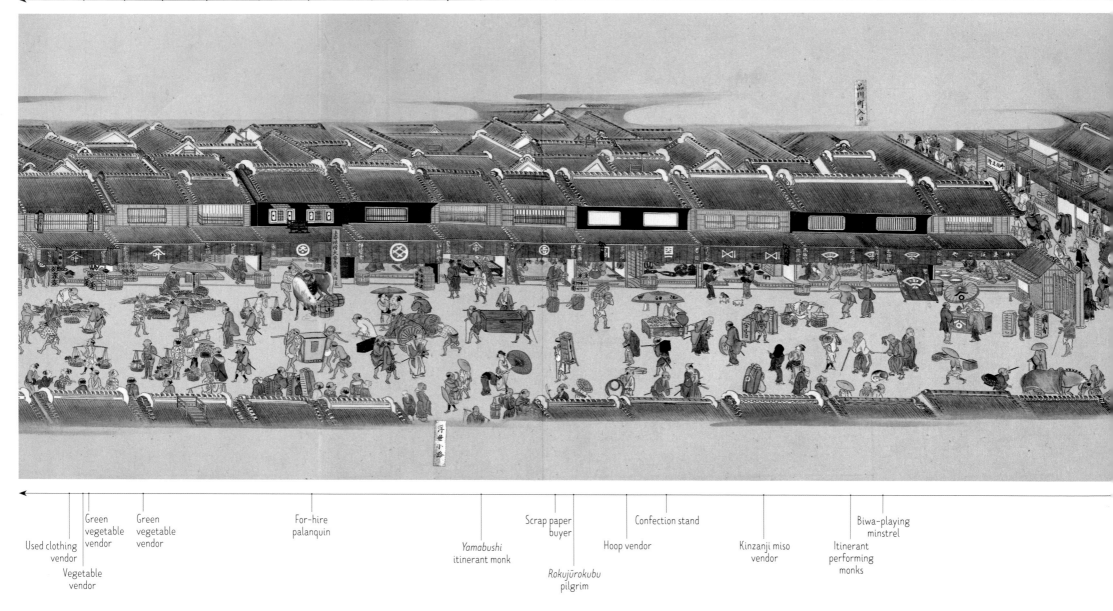

Used clothing
vendor

Green
vegetable
vendor

Green
vegetable
vendor

Vegetable
vendor

For-hire
palanquin

Yamabushi
itinerant monk

Rokujūrokubu
pilgrim

Scrap paper
buyer

Hoop vendor

Confection stand

Kinzanji miso
vendor

Itinerant
performing
monks

Biwa-playing
minstrel

Mount Fuji

Ikkokubashi Bridge

Edo Castle

Nihonbashi Bridge

Entrance to Kugidana
(area with stores selling nails and hardware)

Izumiya

Grocery store

Izumoya

Musashiya

Grocery and dry food store (Kanōya)

Town gate

Sake wholesaler (Kamedaya)

Entrance to Honfunachō

Grocery store (Yaoya)

Neighborhood cistern

Accessory wholesaler (Nikkōya)

Neighborhood cistern

Betrothal gift wholesaler (Yorozuya)

Muromachi 1-chōme

Samurai procession

Vegetable vendor

Bringing the catch ashore

Fishmonger

Crowd north of Nihonbashi Bridge

Fishmonger

Vegetable vendor

Vegetable vendor

Fishmonger

Vegetable vendor

Vegetable vendor

Street brawl

Street brawl

Leather *tabi*
socks store

Vegetable
shop

Tsuruya

Notice boards

Details enlarged on the following pages

p. 66   p. 65   p. 63   p. 61   p. 60

Sweets vendor

This street vendor is selling Ōmiya brand sweets. Like the Kiriya vendor in Honchō 2-chōme, he is going all out to gain clients so he can eventually open a store on the main street. There were also Ōmiya confectioneries in Kōjimachi and Koishikawa Hakusanshita. The sweets sold at such mobile stands were made in lanes and back alleys.

Edo branches of provincial medicine shops

This section of the street, a traditional district of medicine wholesalers, was filled with pharmacies and money changers. The hanging sign advertises Ryūkōtan, a medicine whose properties have been lost to the ages. Stores with signs for Hakuyōsan, Kanryōen, and other medicines are local branches of medicine shops from provinces around Japan.

The all-weather "Rain or Shine Store"

Shimaya sold umbrellas and leather-soled sandals. Because the store sold goods for both rainy weather or fair, it became known as Terifuriya, the "Rain or Shine Store." There was also a "Rain or Shine Town" just past the Uogashi fish market, where wholesale stores specializing in sandals and wooden clogs stood alongside those specializing in umbrellas.

Riverside fish cake store

Kamaboko fish cakes were originally fashioned by wrapping the mashed flesh of fish around stalks of bamboo. During the Edo period, it became common to make the cakes by mashing white fish into a paste, then shaping it and steaming till firm. Samurai families used *kamaboko* as gifts.

Miso shop Ōtaya

The miso jars on the roof are conspicuous advertising. The large oblong sign out front says "Fine red miso." This storefront is also done in the black plaster style just coming into vogue, and the shop is proudly prospering.

Black plaster storehouse

This store stands out from the rest for its architectural style: a durable storehouse of earthen walls known as a *dozō*, this one finished with a coat of black plaster. This style was to become hugely popular from the Tenpō era (1830–1844) through the end of the Tokugawa period. Black plaster enhanced the urban landscape by absorbing light, unlike the glare of white plaster.

Hitachiya confectionery

This is the sole confectionery on Nihonbashi Street. One of the biggest observances at Edo Castle in early summer was "Kajō no gi," which involved eating sweets to ward off sickness. The shogun would present sweets as gifts, and this is perhaps the store that made sweets to his order. The confections on display are elegant ones appropriate for gift-giving by the samurai class. Another famous confectionery in the Nihonbashi neighborhood was Kanazawa Tangonojō.

Sake vendor doing a brisk business
In this neighborhood near Nihonbashi
Bridge, people drinking sake sold by this
street vendor are mingled in the crowd.
The lined-up sake bottles seem to offer
a tonic. It's past noon, and the work of
samurai and merchants alike is largely
done, leaving the men free to enjoy a drink
in these peaceful times.

Fights and fires: the "flowers of Edo"
"Now, now . . ." A town official tries
to stop a fight among botefuri, street
vendors who carry their wares on a pole
across their shoulders. Evidently, others
also tried to intervene and got caught
up in the dispute. The argument may
be over a space at the nearby fruit and
vegetable market in Uogashi.

Ornamental railing pillar tops
Only bridges managed directly by the Tokugawa shogunate would have railing tops like this, decorated in the form of a sacred gem shaped like an onion bulb. Apart from the bridge leading into Edo Castle, the only other bridges in the city with this feature were Nihonbashi, Kyōbashi, and Shinbashi.

"Coming through!"
An enormous, bustling mass of people fills the square. Wending their way through the crowds are dashing young men from the fish market, shouldering baskets of fish just acquired from barges at the water's edge. There is no end to the savory accompaniments for *sake* that are being sold here.

石橋

日□

Edo, city of water
On the river below Nihonbashi Bridge
are houseboats and eight-oared
fishing boats. Goods from every corner
of the country are unloaded here,
while children frolic in the warm
waters of the river. The warm season is
a busy one for both people and goods.

A superlative view
Nihonbashi Bridge was a high
arched bridge offering a fine view
of Edo Castle and Mount Fuji. Little
roofs over the extended bridge
girders offered protection against
the elements and helped to prolong
the life of the wooden bridge.

The artist's proud craftsmanship

From the early eighteenth century, there were always five notices at official notice board sites, to inform the public of laws, regulations, and prohibitions issued by the shogunate. The notices were all posted under a roof, but the scroll's artist depicted two boards outside so he would have room to write out the notices in full. The sheltered notice boards are light-colored and the exposed ones are darker, weather-beaten. The attention to such detail is the mark of a playful spirit that captures the essence of this miniature world.

'*That is exactly the purpose that Kidai Shōran serves,* **documenting for us a now-lost quarter of the city and the lives of its inhabitants,** *not one hundred but two hundred years on.* page 100 '

'**Kibyōshi, books weaving local gossip and incidents into stories, were hugely popular . . .** *readers needed to be well versed in social trends and the latest fashions.* page 73 '

Merchants' Favorite Reading: From "How-to" Books to Digests of Great Works
See page 73

Nansō satomi hakkenden (The eight dog chronicles), 106 vols, by Kyokutei Bakin. (Tokyo Metropolitan Foundation for History and Culture Image Archives)

THE NIHONBASHI NEIGHBORHOOD WAS Edo's premium amusement district, lined with theaters offering kabuki, *jōruri* puppet theater, and other entertainment. Before the Tenpō Reforms of 1841–1843, when all theaters were moved to an area near Sensōji temple, there were three great theaters in Edo: Nakamuraza in Sakaichō, Ichimuraza in Fukiyachō, and Moritaza in Kobikichō. A row of playhouses on Ryōgoku's Honchō Street offered diverse forms of entertainment— everything from plays and narration to conjuring tricks and acrobatics.

The most common form of entertainment for Edo townsmen was the theater. For kabuki, the three great theaters were supplemented by smaller ones such as Miyakoza. *Jōruri* puppet theaters were also popular. *Shibaijaya*, "theater teahouses," offered theatergoers food and drink and helped to form the nucleus of theater towns.

Theatrical productions ran all day, from first light until sundown. People would check the program and reserve seats. They could order food from teahouses attached to the theaters and eat and drink while immersing themselves in a world removed from the everyday.

Early kabuki was performed with a stage and floor galleries but no roof, so performances were canceled when it rained. Not until the Kyōho era (1716–1736) did roofs become commonplace. The most expensive seats, those on either side of the floor galleries, were lined with scarlet felt mats and occupied by upper-class townsmen. Viewers occupying box seats in the front pit, called the *hira-doma* ("flat earthen floor"), brought their own matting to sit on. The cheapest gallery seats were those on the first floor, and people sitting there were referred to as *uzura*, "quails," because they craned their necks to see.

The program was fuller than it is today. Playwrights would sometimes rewrite the script in the middle of the performance as they gauged the audience's reaction. *Sogamono* were tales of vengeance and honor, and anecdotes from true stories would often be added to make them more relevant. Plays were staged for days on end in desperate efforts to satisfy audiences that were highly critical of the plots and the actors' abilities.

Kaomise, annual "face-showing" productions, were held at the beginning of the season, in the eleventh lunar month. Prior to that, the main actors were rated, and some were chosen to earn an annual salary of one thousand *ryō*. This gave rise to the expression *senryō yakusha* ("1,000-*ryō* actor") to refer to a star.

Theaters were also a place for social gatherings, including *miai*, the formal introduction to prospective marriage partners for daughters of wealthy merchants. Audiences enjoyed watching not only the actors on stage, but also the beauties who would emerge from an attached teahouse in a change of dress.

Ōshibai hanjō no zu (Pictures of the great theaters prospering), by Toyokuni III. (Tokyo Metropolitan Foundation for History and Culture Image Archives)

Shichidaime Ichikawa Danjūrō shibai esugata Sukeroku (Ichikawa Danjūrō VII in the role of Sukeroku), by Utagawa Toyokuni. (Tokyo Metropolitan Foundation for History and Culture Image Archives)

Merchants learned reading, writing, and abacus calculations through *ōraimono*, primary textbooks in the style of corresponding letters. Also widely read were practical books, such as *Onna daigaku* (Great learning for women, c. 1716), which offered guidance on marriage, childbirth, and other topics important to women, and *Yōjōkun* (Precepts for the preservation of health, 1712), both by the Neo-Confucianist philosopher Kaibara Ekiken (1630–1714).

Educational books included Confucian texts such as *Great Learning*, the *Analects*, *Doctrine of the Mean*, and *Mencius*, as well as their digest versions. Poetry was absorbed through commentaries on *waka* and *Hyakunin isshu* ("One hundred poets, one poem each"). Among women readers, *Kogetsushō* ("The moon on the lake"), a commentary on *The Tale of Genji*, was a runaway bestseller.

As the publishing industry grew, low-priced books became popular with the common people. *Kusazōshi* were small ten-page booklets approximately the size of modern Japanese paperbacks. Each page had a woodblock illustration, so they were also called *ezōshi*, "picture books." The booklets were works of fiction, color coded by genre. Red-covered *akahon* featured children's stories, including folktales and fairy tales like "Peach Boy" and "The Mouse's Wedding." Blue-covered *aohon* offered more sophisticated storybooks for adults, consisting of retellings of plots from the puppet theater and kabuki. *Kibyōshi*, yellow-covered books weaving local gossip and incidents into stories, were hugely popular.

Authors of *kibyōshi* included daimyō

retainers and vassals of the shogun, typified by Hōseidō Kisanji (1735–1813), a high commissioner in Edo under the Satake domain of Akita. (Kisanji also wrote satirical *kyōka*, "mad verse," under the pen name Tegarano Okamochi.) Cultured townsmen such as Santō Kyōden were also masters of the genre.

To appreciate the parodies created by such men of culture, readers needed to be well versed in social trends and the latest fashions. *Kibyōshi* appealed greatly to Edoites' sense of humor, but eventually fell into decline following the Publishing Control Ordinance issued during the Kansei Reforms of 1787 to 1793.

The common people also loved *kokkeibon* (humorous books) like *Shank's Mare* by Jippensha Ikku (1765–1831) and *The Bathhouse of the Floating World* by Shikitei Sanba (1776–1822), as well as *yomihon* (reading books) like *The Eight Dog Chronicles* by Kyokutei Bakin (1767–1848). These came in deluxe editions containing advertisements and illustrations. As the tales were simultaneously featured in kabuki plays and *kōshaku* (public storytelling or narration), they connected readers to a diverse world while allowing them to enjoy new dramas.

Suharaya and the other major publishing houses on Nihonbashi Street also published a variety of maps and the latest information from Nagasaki, Japan's window on the West. People living in Nihonbashi shops, large and small, could read newly published books by renting them from a book-lending shop. When necessary, they could transcribe the books by hand to keep them for handy reference.

Merchants' Favorite Reading:

From "How-To" Books to Digests of Great Works

Shūgyoku bukan (A directory of samurai officialdom), published by Suharaya Mohei. (Tokyo Metropolitan Foundation for History and Culture Image Archives)

Occupations and Arts Illustrated in
Kidai Shōran

The street rings with vibrant sounds:
Cries of vendors selling sushi, miso, water, medicine, tobacco, pipes, used clothing . . .
Merchants' greetings
Bells ringing the hour

A variety of aromas fill the air:
Savory roasted rice cakes
Sweet red-bean soup
Miso and soy sauce
Vinegared rice
Hair oil, rouge, and powder
Medicines from Southeast Asia
Musk and sandalwood

A Guide to Occupations and Arts Illustrated in Kidai Shōran

All sorts of workers thronged Nihonbashi Street, the liveliest place in old Edo: peddlers selling stock to wholesalers, hawkers heading for clients in the back alleys, street vendors conspicuously placed, repairmen setting up shop, itinerant musicians and entertainers performing in front of the large stores . . .

Knife sharpener and knife repairman

The knife sharpener would sharpen any cutting tool other than swords, including kitchen knives, spades, and hoes. The repairman would hone a chipped blade on a rough whetstone, then patch and braze as required.

Samurai palanquin

Palanquins required two or four bearers. Men only rode in them if they were of quite high rank. In town, they were used mostly by women. *Onna norimono*, palanquins used by upper-class women, were decorated on the outside with *makie* (gold and silver decorations on lacquer) and metal ornaments, and on the inside with scenes from *The Tale of Genji* or the *Tales of Ise*, paintings of flowers and birds, and the like.

Pottery vendors

One vendor unpacks bowls just arrived from the country, while another sets off to hawk his wares. Imari ware, Arita ware, Kutani ware: many famous styles were named for their place of production, but so much pottery came from Seto in present-day Aichi prefecture that the word *setomono* became a generic term for pottery. Seto produced so much pottery that people switched from using wooden vessels for daily use.

Confection stand

The vendor would dip dumplings
into the jug of syrup and then wrap
them in a sheet of the paper hanging
from the umbrella before handing
them to the customer. The street
was always thronged, and many
stalls like this tempted passersby
with rice cakes, candy, rice crackers,
and other snacks.

Oxcart

In Edo districts, daimyō estates, temples, and
shrines were located on hilltops, and bridges
were arched, so lumber, stone, sacks of rice,
and other heavy loads were transported by
large two-wheeled carts, hand-drawn or ox-
drawn. Horses were ridden by samurai and
generally not harnessed in town, although
sometimes they were used to transport rice
or people long distances.

Cobbler

Zōri sandals of cloth or rice straw could
be easily discarded, but sandals made of
woven rush, like tatami mats, and lined
with leather soles were high-class footwear
worn by samurai and shopkeepers. When
the thongs or soles were worn out or
damaged, they were repaired. Walking
on streets of dirt or gravel made regular
maintenance essential.

Medicine vendor

No two signboards of medicine wholesalers in Nihonbashi Honchō have the same name for a medicine. Each store was the exclusive Edo outlet for the medicine made by its patron. This man may be hawking medicine from his hometown.

Sushi vendor

The most common types of sushi at this time were pressed sushi and *inarizushi* (pouches of fried tofu filled with rice). Sushi removed from the mold and cut into squares was packed in boxes and hawked on the street. Modern hand-rolled sushi, also known as *Edomaezushi* ("Edo-style sushi"), first became popular in the Bunsei era (1818–1830) as an inexpensive fast food sold at stalls.

Book lender

Books were expensive, so people relied on book lenders to bring new books around. Merchants who catered to samurai households sought books on heraldry, paper cutting, lists of shogunate offices, and the like, while merchants' daughters waited eagerly for the latest popular books, such as *Kogetsushō* (Moonlight on the lake), a commentary on *The Tale of Genji*.

Kindling vendor

Tsukegi were 6-inch pieces of cedar or cypress kindling treated with phosphorous on one side so they would catch fire right away. A precursor of today's matches.

Couriers

If you took an item marked with a name and address to a transfer station, it would be faithfully delivered to its destination. Private courier companies had to join a merchant guild. Edo couriers made thrice-monthly deliveries and were connected to similar operations in Osaka and Kyoto through relay stations. Besides letters, couriers delivered parcels, goods, and cash. Often, one man would carry the letter while another rang a bell or shouted to clear the way.

Street-stall teahouse

A teahouse in the middle of a heavily trafficked road was a year-round respite for pedestrians, something like an open-air café today. The checkered roof and the benches could all be quickly disassembled and folded up for easy mobility. A woman with her hair in the "lantern sidelocks" style then in vogue is serving tea.

Fish and *sake* delivery

Fresh fish just in at the Uogashi fish market were swiftly transported to clients in baskets suspended from a shoulder pole. *Sake* was measured from a barrel and sold by the amount. The delivery boy wearing a workman's apron is carrying a two-handled keg in one hand and a list of his customers and what they owe in the other.

Bird catcher

The bird catcher could enter any estate in the city on the pretext of catching birds to feed the shogun's falcons. The *torimi*, or officer for falconry, had the right to enter estate grounds on inspections in advance of the shogun's hawking expeditions. This was also a way of spying on the daimyō.

Rokujūrokubu pilgrims

Also known as *rokubu*, these pilgrims would travel to sixty-six sacred sites around the country, shouldering a Buddhist statue and chanting an homage to the Lotus Sutra—"*Namu myōhō rengekyō*"— on their way. At each site they would donate hand-copied portions of the sutra. If their money ran out, they would offer prayers and receive alms. Some, though, undertook the pilgrimage as a way to flee their village after having committed a crime.

Rice polisher

He walks along carrying a long-handled pestle and rolling a mortar in front of him, ready to polish rice if asked. In winter, he pounds glutinous rice into mochi rice cakes. People living in back alleys appreciated this service, as they didn't have room for the necessary equipment for polishing. Such services show the convenience of city living at the time.

Street palanquin

The street palanquin (*tsujikago*), so named because its operators touted on street corners, was a mode of transportation used by townsmen going to or from the pleasure quarters or on longer trips. Most were simple, like this one, and were also known as four-handed or hanging palanquins. Passengers had to be patient, and the ride was not very comfortable.

Senior priest

He seems to be selling amulets from Ise Grand Shrine. The bell is perhaps to invoke a deity. Priests traveled from Ise to Edo to sell charms, as the people of Edo were particularly drawn to Ise Shrine. Many people in the city had come from Ise, as indicated by the large number of shops styled "Iseya." The proprietor of Mitsui Echigoya was also from there. There was a large shrine in Shinkawa.

Lacquerer

This lacquerer is plying his trade on the main thoroughfare. One might think a lacquerer would want to avoid dust at any cost, but perhaps he came out from a back-alley tenement for the light. There were a number of shops and wholesalers dealing in lacquerware in this neighborhood.

Monkey trainer

A dog barks at the monkey on the trainer's back, illustrating the expression "to get on like dogs and monkeys" (to be on bad terms). Monkeys were the clowns of an ancient circus-like form of entertainment introduced from China in the eighth century, and were said to protect samurai horses from *kappa*, mythical river imps. Shows featuring trained monkeys were a popular form of street entertainment from the fifteenth century, but around this time, people in the nobility and the military class kept monkeys as pets.

Pipe vendor

A great many pipe vendors like this one appear in the scroll painting, perhaps indicating a connection to the artist Santō Kyōden, who ran a shop in Kyōbashi selling tobacco pouches. Or perhaps the prosperous pipe store of Nakamuraya Genpachi was among the sponsors of the *Kidai Shōran* scroll.

Water vendor

He offers drinking water, freshly drawn from a city well in wooden buckets, to refresh thirsty people on the busy street. In an earlier era, vendors sold "a cup for a copper" (*ippuku issen*) and medicinal tea. In hot weather, this vendor might also offer loquat-leaf tea or watermelon or other fruit to ward off the heat.

Young Mitsui Echigoya workers

The Mitsui Echigoya store in Edo was run by employees hailing from Kyoto. Their course of advancement was clear: they started out as *kodomo*, apprentices; on coming of age at around eighteen, they became *wakashu*, with increased responsibility, then *tedai*, salesclerks. Boys around the age pictured were eager for *hatsunobori*, their first home visit after entering the Edo store's employ.

Hoop vendor

Buckets, pails, barrels, dining tables, and other items were repaired by splitting bamboo and fashioning it into hoops of the appropriate size. When barrels and buckets held together by hoops began to be made around the end of the fifteenth century, the brewing industry, which had been using earthenware jars, was able to engage in large-scale production, and business boomed.

Bamboo ware vendor

Sieves, baskets, miso strainers . . . all sorts of bamboo wares were sold. Items made of woven bamboo were used in various facets of daily life, each with its particular use. Their tight weave ensured they would last for years.

Toy vendor

Tree-climbing monkeys, toy drums, and other children's playthings are for sale. Red Inari flags were popular not only as toys but as talismans to protect children from sickness and evil.

Incantation chanter

Many religious people probably came to this bustling center of the capital to proselytize, and a man like this would chant prayers and incantations as a kind of strolling performance. Superstitious merchants could not take a chance on turning away anyone who offered prayers on their behalf.

Kinzanji miso vendor

Kinzanji was a miso brand of Chinese origin. The Zen priest Kakushin (1207–1298) is said to have spread the manufacturing method on his return from Jingshan temple in China. This miso was served as an accompaniment to *sake*. The vendor would shout out a list of his offerings as he walked about.

Kokubu tobacco vendor

The *chinko-kiri* tobacco vendor went about selling finely cut leaf tobacco, a different brand in each drawer. As Kokubu, in Kagoshima province, was the most famous center of tobacco production, "Kokubu" became synonymous with tobacco sellers. Edoites enjoyed the luxury of purchasing aromatic, freshly cut tobacco in small amounts to smoke as they pleased.

Maruichi *daikagura* circus troupe

This troupe of performing artists juggled and did balancing acts using umbrellas and sticks, as well as doing the lion dance, showing escape artistry using cylindrical baskets, and so on. *Daikagura* circus performance originated when representatives of Atsuta Shrine in Nagoya, Aichi prefecture, traveled around the country performing the lion dance and distributing talismans. In time, the religious aspect diminished, and the acts became popular entertainment. The Maruichi troupe was famous in Edo, and the thirteenth-generation head of the troupe remains active today.

Used clothing vendor

The man is selling used clothing and pieces of cloth from dismantled kimono. Used clothing had many uses. It was the everyday wear of common people, including servants in large merchant houses. The wooden pole the vendor has draped his merchandise over could be adapted to sell other goods by hanging a wooden plate from either end.

Vegetable vendor

The vendor is selling what appear to be bamboo shoots, arranged in a row. Bamboo shoots from Meguro were prized. Bamboo shoots are harvested in early spring, and this—along with the depiction of the doll fair in early March and scenes of children playing in the river—suggests that *Kidai Shōran* is set in the spring and summer.

Green vegetable vendor

Vendors would go to the vegetable markets in Tachō and Saekichō in the Kanda district and stock up on eggplants, *daikon* radishes, and green vegetables. They sold their produce from baskets hanging from a pole. The vendors rubbed shoulders as they went back and forth in the bustling neighborhood of Muromachi 1-chōme.

Scrap paper buyer

This man is using a scale to weigh the scrap paper he has just purchased. All kinds of scrap paper were sought: old account records, letters, news sheets, books. Handmade *washi* paper was recycled into new paper.

A Guided Tour Through *Kidai Shōran*

On a mild spring day in 1805, a genial retiree guides us down Nihonbashi Street.

Imagawabashi Bridge

There's a haiku stanza that goes, "Imagawabashi Bridge is a dinky little bridge," and it's true. It's a small bridge over the Kanda canal, apparently named after a town chief who lived nearby.

In Edo neighborhoods, wholesale dealers in the same business traditionally cluster together, and that's why you see a lot of pottery wholesalers on both sides of the bridge here. You'll find pottery from Kutani, Arita, and Seto that has come to Edo Bay and been transferred onto flatboats to come up the shallow canal. Right here is a good place to unload it.

That store with a logo of concentric circles on its shop curtain and banner sells malt sugar. It's only lately that you find a shop like that right in the middle of the pottery district. A sign of the times. One of the pottery wholesalers went out of business, and a malt-sugar dealer moved in.

Honshiroganechō Street

To the right of the town gate is the checkpoint, and on the left is the guardhouse. Honshiroganechō Street is the cross street here. Way down at the end of the street is Edo Castle, and in the opposite direction is Kodenmachō prison and execution ground.

You'll notice an awful lot of dogs on this street. You know what they say Edo is famous for? Ise merchants, Inari shrines, and dog shit. Everywhere you go, you'll see stores labeled "Iseya," Inari shrines, and plenty of dog shit. Watch out! See? You almost stepped in it.

We meet at the south edge of Imagawabashi Bridge in Kanda . . .

Well, well! So you're a traveler who's come to Edo all the way from western Japan, are you? Then you'll have left Kyoto on the Tōkaidō highway, changed at the Kusatsu crossroad to the Nakasendō highway and passed through the Kiso valley, deep in the mountains. You must have passed Lake Suwa and Mount Asama before coming to the crossroad in Hongō, where you connected to the Nikkō Onari Kaidō highway leading to Edo.

I'll bet you crossed the river Kanda on Shōheibashi Bridge. Or maybe you went over Sujikaibashi Bridge instead, before going through Sujikai Gate to Yatsukōji. The crowds at Sujikaibashi Bridge were lively, weren't they? That's been a transportation hub since Edo's first days.

Before I show you around Nihonbashi, let's have a cup of tea at this teahouse by the foot of the bridge, shall we? It's been here for ages. This whole section of Edo, west of the north side of the bridge, used to be called Monto Bank. That's because Okubo Monto, who dug a well in Edo two hundred years ago, lived near here. Monto's Well, they called it. The water is supposed to have been very pure, just right for the tea ceremony. All the travelers to Edo enter the city here, not just those coming on the Nakasendō from your area, but people from every part of the country.

Nihonbashi Bridge is straight ahead, at the other end of the street—about 760 meters from here. How long will it take us to get there? Well, if we take our time, about an hour, I'd say. But don't worry. I'm retired now, with all the time in the world. I sent the clerk who was with me back to the store, so I'll be happy to escort you all the way down the street.

Have you finished your tea? Right, then, shall we be off?

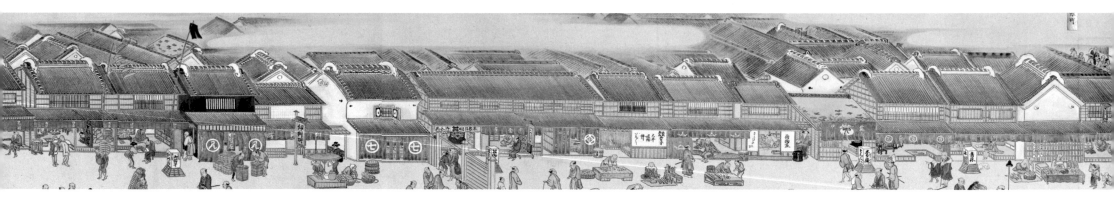

Honkokuchō 2-chōme (north)

This is the gate marking the border between Honshiroganechō and Honkokuchō. Across the street is the "Bell of Time." Bashō's famous line, "Is it the bell in Ueno or Asakusa?" refers to the Kan'eiji temple bell on Ueno hill and the one in Asakusa's Sensōji temple. But the first such bell was the one installed here in Honkokuchō—though originally it was in Edo Castle, they say.

The bell ringer first strikes the bell three times to draw people's attention, and then he strikes the time. He does it every two hours, morning and night, so it's a tough job. The bell hanging there now was recast in 1711. Listen—there it goes now.

There are nine bells in Edo, and people living within range of the sound pay a certain amount to support the bell ringer. The Honkokuchō bell has a wide range. They say it carries east as far as the Sumida River, south to Hamachō in Shiba, west to Iidamachi and Kōjimachi, and north to Hongō 6-chōme.

The Nagasakiya inn, over there on the north corner of Honkokuchō 3-chōme, is where Dutch traders stay when they come to Edo from Dejima in Nagasaki. They come every time there's a new shogun, of course. And they're required to come and submit reports on world news at regular intervals. When that happens, this place really gets packed with people who flock here to catch a glimpse of red-headed, blue-eyed Dutchmen. Scholars come, too, hoping to see the books and goods they bring with them.

The Korean delegations always lodge in Asakusa at Higashi Honganji temple, which is famous for the massive roof of its main hall.

Honshiroganechō 2-chōme

The town sections are numbered by how close they are to the castle, with 1-chōme being the closest. There've always been bookstores from here to Nihonbashi Bridge, right from the start. Publishers from Kyoto and Osaka that represent the picture book and print publishers guild came here to open stores. I'd say the most influential name in publishing now is Suharaya. Here you see Suharaya Zengorō, and up ahead in Muromachi 2-chōme there's Suharaya Ichibei, a publisher and bookseller.

See those signs advertising *The Works of Ogyū Sorai* and *Collected Haikai*? Suharaya Ichibei also published that famous book called the *New Book of Anatomy*, translated by Sugita Genpaku, in 1774. That became a bestseller, you know. The illustrations were by Odano Naotake, a retainer of Kakunodate in Akita province who painted what they called *ranga*, Dutch-style paintings.

Look over there. That's Fujiya, selling *shiruko mochi*, the sweet bean porridge with mochi rice cakes, and *zōni*, broth with rice cakes and vegetables. A small shop for such a famous place, isn't it? In fact, that's the only one-story building on Nihonbashi Street roofed with wood shingles instead of tile. After the previous store went under, someone in the food business snapped up the property because of its prime location. *Shiruko mochi* and *zōni* both sell for 12 *mon* (¥300 in today's currency).

You've probably noticed that the stores facing Nihonbashi Street have some fine roof tiles. At first, townsfolk weren't allowed to have tiled roofs at all, except for three-story turrets on prominent corner properties. But after the Great Meireki Fire of 1657, when even the keep of Edo Castle burned down, people began to argue that tiles were necessary to fireproof buildings. Still, the authorities forbade their use because they cost too much. Finally, in 1720, they started encouraging the use of *dozō-zukuri* (mud-covered walls finished with plaster), *nuriya-zukuri* (lacquered walls) and tiled roofs. Before you knew it, wood shingles and thatch were forbidden, and roofs *had* to be tiled.

Now, almost all the stores here are two stories with a tiled roof. Three-story buildings were prohibited in 1649, and people matched the height of their eaves with their neighbors. See how all the houses are beautifully aligned?

Honkokuchō 2-chōme (south)

This area has stores selling textiles from Kyoto and Osaka or cloth and paper imported from China. They also sell Buddhist robes, rolls of cotton, pongee, Kyoto thread, and paper for *fusuma* doors. Currency exchanges, pharmacies, and booksellers used to be the main businesses on Nihonbashi Street, but the city consumes so much paper and clothing that the number of these stores has gone way up. In the last fifty years, there's been an influx of all sorts of businesses. Another sign of the times.

Yes, there are lots of tenements on the back streets. But the ones here are relatively high-priced compared to those across the river in Fukagawa or Hatchōbori. The tenants are mostly artisans and other workers, or clerks from the big stores who want to live near their workplace. They can get all the fresh food they could possibly want from the fish and vegetable markets. Cosmetics from Kyoto and other items they might want are also right at hand. They don't even have to go inside the stores, because there are plenty of stalls on the main street, and the side streets are full of people hawking various things. People who live here get to enjoy all the conveniences of city life, believe me.

Honkokuchō Street

Go west on this street and you'll come to the Edo Castle moat. Go east and you'll pass through Kodenmachō to the Asakusa Gate. The street runs straight all the way from the castle to Asakusabashi Bridge, in other words. If you go through Kuramae, past the giant rice warehouse where the stipends of Tokugawa retainers are paid out, you'll come to the Kozukappara execution grounds, with Sensōji temple and the Yoshiwara pleasure quarters to one side. Cross Senjuōhashi Bridge and you'll find yourself on the Ōshū road, branching off from the Nikkō road and leading north to Mito.

See the *tobi* guard in front of the checkpoint? At first, the store owners who were responsible for the town's financial ledgers would take turns at guard duty, but as they were often too busy to handle the responsibility, the town began to hire *tobi* as vigilantes. They also help out as firefighters.

Honchō 2-chōme (north)

Look at all the medicine wholesalers here on Honchō and Nihonbashi Streets. I heard that Shikitei Sanba, the famous writer of popular fiction, wants to set up shop at the end of that street to sell patent medicines. They say he's going to call the store Shikitei Seiho, and he's thinking of selling his own aromatic water, "Edo Water." He'll put it in glass bottles, pack them each in a paulownia-wood box, and sell the boxes for 48 *mon* apiece (¥1200 in today's currency). Might make a good souvenir of Edo at that. Sounds like a guaranteed hit to me.

As we've been walking along, have you looked up at all? Did you notice the fire watchtowers and weather vanes on the store rooftops? Remember, this is a city of frequent fires, and there are so many large stores here that a fire would be disastrous. When the fire bell rings, people race to the watchtower to see which way the flames are headed. If the wind is blowing their way, a plasterer soon comes running.

When fire threatens, plasterers close the storehouse doors and windows and seal them. If there's no lime on hand, they use miso paste. The items of greatest value are stored in underground cellars. Large stores around here have more than one cellar for storage. Rainwater cisterns aren't enough in case of fire, so scattered all around town are water barrels filled with city water for firefighting.

Jikkendana

Ah, here we have one of the great signs of spring in Edo. The Jikkendana Doll Fair is held about ten days before the Doll Festival in March. It started out with about ten temporary stalls set up with straw mats on either side of the street—that's how it got its name, which means "ten stores." There are fairs for the Boys' Festival in May and at the end of the year, too. You've timed your visit perfectly. Why not buy a pair of emperor and empress dolls for your granddaughter?

Oh, there's an empty store. It opened for business here in the center of town, but something must've gone wrong. Well, businesses tend to come and go in Edo. Life has its ups and downs, and that's just how it is. Still, any empty place in this neighborhood will soon find a new tenant, since you hardly ever see vacancies. Lots of the landlords don't live around here. Having an Edo store to let out is a sign of wealth in the provinces, you see. Then they leave supervision to a *yamori*, someone hired to manage things in their absence.

How much is the rent? Not all that high. Even so, one of the back tenements in the Nihonbashi area would run you 4 *momme* of silver per *tsubo*—about four times what it would be anywhere else. Two rooms, one an earthen-floor room with a hearth, about 3 *tsubo* in all, would be about 12 *momme*. In coin, that's 1,200 *mon*, the price of a hundred bowls of *zōni* at that shop we passed earlier. Closer to the main street, of course, the rent might be two or two-and-a-half times higher. I've heard that for a corner residence in Ōdenmachō, it's even higher—more than 20 *momme* per *tsubo*.

Honchō 2-chōme (south)

The corner store with the bright red banner is the famous Tamaya, a wholesale dealer in rouge and powder. They also handle aromatic aloeswood oil, which is very popular now. It's even mentioned in Sanba's popular book, *Bathhouse of the Floating World*.

Can you smell the aloeswood? A fine fragrance, isn't it?

Up ahead is Nakamuraya, the pipe dealer. They'll make you a pipe to order. The quality is far better than what you get from the hawkers in the street. For leaf tobacco, you can go to Ōtaya, which we passed a moment ago. Kokubu tobacco vendors come by here fairly often, too.

Thanks to the guardhouse at the entrance to every neighborhood, Edo is a pretty safe city. The gates open around six in the morning and generally close up around ten at night, though I've heard they're getting lax lately. If the guard knows you, he'll let you through the side gate. Physicians and midwives have a free pass, any time of night or day.

When the guard lets someone through at night, he strikes wooden clappers to let the next guard know someone is on the way.

Honchō Street

Quite a busy place, eh? This is where you can see processions with samurai in palanquins. It's the most prominent part of this prominent part of town—easily the most prestigious street in all Edo. *Hatamoto* and *gokenin*, the upper and lower retainers of the Tokugawa house, take this route on their way to Edo Castle, heading for Tokiwabashi Gate.

The street is lined with clothing stores and pharmacies. If a merchant from Ise or Oumi opens a store here, it'll make him one of the leading merchants in the capital. Mitsui Echigoya used to be located here. But not far away, just ahead, is an even busier part of Nihonbashi. In other words, Honchō may be prestigious for the samurai class, but merchants have made Surugachō the business center of Nihonbashi, where they make money hand over fist.

Surugachō Street

This is the Mitsui Echigoya, the biggest store in all Edo, dealing in kimono and money exchange. Did you ever see so many customers in one place? It all started just 120 years ago. Mitsui Takatoshi, a businessman from Matsusaka in the province of Ise, was successful in Kyoto; he moved his Edo shop here from Honchō in 1683. His policy of "cash only, prices as advertised" was a big hit.

This is the busiest section of Nihonbashi Street. The saying goes that thousands of *ryō* change hands here every day.

Notice the gate is made of plain wood. Normally they're covered black with persimmon tannin, but not the ones by main streets.

Straight down this street, in Honryōgaechō, is the shogunate's gold mint. No wonder this area has always been Edo's financial center, with plenty of money changers.

Muromachi 3-chōme

Now we're in another area with lots of pharmacies and cosmetics stores. See the Tawaraya signboard advertising a "wonder drug for underarm odor?" Do you suppose it works?

And look at that load of goods that's just arrived at Kagiya. It's stamped with *goku*, a kind of permit required for transporting goods, so it must have come from Kyoto.

Oh yes, the residence of Edo's leading city elder is in this neighborhood, too. Official notices from the magistrate's office are conveyed first to the city elders, then to the town chiefs, then the landlords, and through them to tenants in back alleys. That's how information spreads. In Muromachi 3-chōme we have the residence of Kitamura, in Honchō 2-chōme it's Taruya, and in Honchō 1-chōme it's Naraya. Their positions are hereditary, going back generations.

The little road ahead on the east side is called Ukiyo Shōji, "Floating World Lane." Why the fancy name? Because long ago, they used to sell something there called *ukiyo goza*, "floating-world mats." They were all the rage at the time.

Oh, wait . . . See the nicely dressed woman in lacquered sandals heading into the Yorozuya cloth wholesaler? She's a geisha and no mistake. The man following her is a dashing *hakoya*, and it's his job to carry her shamisen.

Take a look at the sign in front of the abacus shop Sashimaya, in the shape of a big abacus. It's really well made, and there are even two beads on the upper deck. It was no easy task making an abacus that big, believe you me. It went up just five years ago, in May 1800. Since it was going to be on a public street, the owner, Sashimaya Chōkichi, had to get permission from the southern magistrate's office. It's heavy and a good 6.3 meters high, so it took 180 men to set it up. They had to lay a good foundation to support it. The magistrate came for inspection, along with the town managers, so it turned into quite an extravaganza.

Shinagawachō Street

Close as we are to the city center, this street has a cluttered look, doesn't it? There's even laundry hanging out to dry. A lot of stores hereabouts sell daily necessities, so when you step away from the main street into a side street like this, you get a glimpse of ordinary life.

There are no fire watchtowers here, so the little bell hanging in the guardhouse serves the purpose of a fire alarm. Only the gatekeeper is allowed to strike it.

Muromachi 1-chōme

We're getting close to Nihonbashi Bridge now, so the street is crowded with peddlers, and the air is thick with their cries. They can't set up shop anywhere they like; there's an agency in charge of who gets what space. Because the fish and produce markets are nearby, the peddlers and the stores used to squabble over access. Then the town divided up the area among 160 peddlers and sold the rights to each location. But don't ask me whether the rent money goes to the townsfolk or the stores—because I don't know.

You'll find a lot of stores around here that cater to the samurai class. Some sell *kamaboko* fish cakes for gifts, some sell betrothal gifts, and others specialize in samurai equipment.

Because of this, we never forget that Edo is a city of samurai.

There's a miso store called Ōtaya, advertising "fine red miso at a low, low price" on the sign in front. All the miso stores used to be in Kanda and Hongō. But the population boom has caused a huge influx of stores selling everyday foods like salt, soy sauce, and miso. Nowadays, locally produced miso and soy sauce support the population of Edo.

Oh, yes—south of here is the neighborhood of Anjinchō, where the sixteenth-century English ship pilot William Adams once lived in a house given to him by the shogun, Tokugawa Ieyasu.

Muromachi 2-chōme

The Mitsui Echigoya conglomerate has stores on both sides of Surugachō Street. In Edo, just as in Kyoto, structures are taxed based on their main-street frontage, so while Mitsui's façade on Nihonbashi Street is narrow, the store extends far down Surugachō Street. Now that's a smart use of space!

The store is nice to look at, don't you think? Its *namakokabe* walls are covered with square tiles that are jointed with white plaster. It has long, indigo shop curtains, copper rain gutters, and reddish latticework. This is the only store on the street that has copper rain gutters.

You might recall that, along the way, we've seen several shops built in the fireproof *dozō-zukuri* style finished with black plaster. That style for buildings fronting the street just recently started gaining in popularity. It takes time and money to apply black plaster, and if you ask me, good old white plaster is prettier. I wonder what made people develop a taste for the color black? Perhaps it means some kind of a black cloud is starting to hang over society. . . .

Anyway, over there at the Kiya store, which is under construction, there's a sign saying "Open for business at the storehouse." They don't close for business even while remodeling. That's the spirit that keeps their business growing, I expect. They've brought hewn stones for the foundation, so the construction will be solid.

Right now, they're putting up the pillars and leveling the ground. You can hear the *tobi* workers calling cheerfully to one another and chanting *kiyari*, a workmen's chant. Their energy is contagious, don't you think?

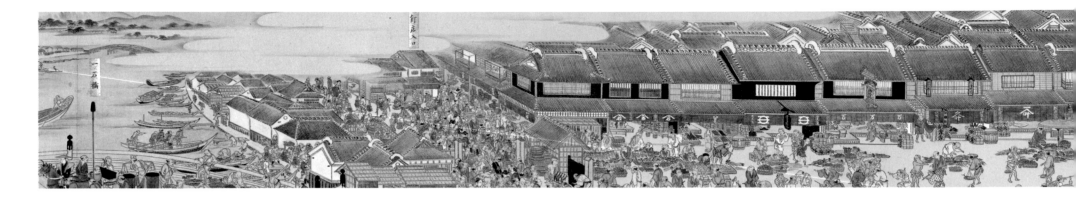

Nihonbashi Bridge, the north side

Well, now, it seems we've come to Nihonbashi Bridge, where the land routes and sea routes all meet in Edo. Here are the finest markets—wholesalers, retailers, and peddlers all come here to stock up on fresh seafood and produce. It's like a year-end fair every day of the year. You've got to look sharp or you'll miss out, because everybody's very serious about business.

Come on, let's stand in the middle of the bridge. Look around: from here you can enjoy the finest views in Edo, from snow-capped Mount Fuji to Edo Castle, where the shogun lives.

On a sadder note, you should be able to see a signpost next to Ichikokubashi Bridge that says, "Lost children." That's where people go to find clues to the whereabouts of missing loved ones, particularly from the frequent fires. There's a similar location in the Sensōji temple compound.

And with that, traveler, I bid you farewell. Have a safe journey, and enjoy the rest of your stay in Edo.

Shiki no yukikai (The changing seasons), text by Santō Kyōden, drawings by Kitao Shigemasa. (National Diet Library)

See page 98

More about the Picture Scroll *Kidai Shōran*

by
Kobayashi Tadashi

I FIRST LEARNED OF THE EXISTENCE OF THE picture scroll *Kidai Shōran* early in the summer of 1999. At the time, I was giving a series of talks on Japanese art in four cities in Germany and Switzerland.

The day after my talk in Cologne, Franziska Ehmcke visited me in the hotel where I was staying. She brought with her detailed photographs of the picture scroll and asked my opinion. Professor Ehmcke is an old acquaintance, a professor of Japanese cultural studies at Cologne University, and she once interpreted for a talk I gave to the Frankfurt Japanese-German Society. At a glance I could see that the work was a late-Tokugawa genre painting of a street scene in the city of Edo. She told me it was being kept in the Museum of East Asian Art, Berlin, and I promised to examine it closely the following week and report my findings to her.

After visiting the Rietberg Museum in Zurich, I delivered my scheduled lecture at the Free University of Berlin, and the next day went to the Museum of East Asian Art, Berlin in Dahlem. The museum director, Prof. Willibald Veit, and the Japanese art curator Dr. Khanh Trinh brought the scroll out of storage along with other works I had asked to examine. Dr. Veit, a Chinese art specialist, explained that the scroll had been donated to the museum by a certain individual and asked me for my evaluation.

He was fully aware of the work's historical value and had already asked Professor Ehmcke to study its content. Now he wanted me to gauge its place in art history.

I spread open the scroll and was astonished at the vivid detail of the Edo townscape and the people going about their daily lives. I remember assuring the director that the work was as precious for its artistry as for its historical value.

The cover was decorated in an auspicious pattern of tortoises and cranes, woven in gold brocade on a ground of blue. On the gold paper label were the words "Kidai Shōran Ten" (Excellent view of this prosperous age, vol. 1). If this were a *ten* ("heaven") volume, there must have also been a *chi* ("earth") volume and possibly a *jin* ("human") volume as well. I asked if they knew of similar picture scrolls somewhere, companions to the one before us. This was the only one, they said, so at some point the set must have been broken up.

I gazed at the scroll, drawn in to the depiction of the great street of Nihonbashi, starting with Imagawabashi Bridge in Kanda and ending with Nihonbashi Bridge. My eyes followed the enormous realism of the bustling scenes, the variety of shops and street stalls, the people of every status and occupation imaginable coming and going in the street. I felt as if I were walking among them.

Who painted Kidai Shōran?

The style of scroll painting seen in *Kidai Shōran*, in which two sides of a street are portrayed at the top and bottom and the scene unfolds horizontally, has a long history. Two early examples are *Tohi zukan* (Picture scroll of town and country; Konbu-in, Nara), a portrayal of scenes in and around Kyoto by Sumiyoshi Gukei (1631–1705), and *Hokurō oyobi engeki zukan* (Picture scroll of the northern brothels [Yoshiwara] and theaters; Tokyo National Museum), a ukiyoe style work by Hishikawa Moronobu (1618–1694).

The composition of *Kidai Shōran* is simply magnificent. In a scroll over 12 meters long, the scene unfolds cinematically, as if a movie camera is panning right to left at a steady pace, leading up to a climactic, noisy quarrel in the crowd swarming about Nihonbashi Bridge and concluding with serene, celebratory images of Edo Castle and Mount Fuji. This remarkable work is a mature urban genre painting of unmatched originality.

The hundreds of people in the painting are drawn with life and color, their movements and posture differentiated in endless variation by gender, age, status, and role. The fluidity of the brush strokes, and the ease and familiarity with which the human figure is rendered, strongly suggest that the painter was someone in the ukiyo-e school. Yet his name is unknown. Not even his seal is on the painting, although perhaps it was on one of the missing scrolls. Identifying the artist by his style is not easy, either. Ukiyo-e scholar Asano Shugō has suggested it could be Katsukawa Shun'ei (1762–1819), but is careful to add that the attribution cannot be definite at this stage (*Ōedo Nihonbashi emaki*, Kodansha, 2003.) I, too, would like to wait and not rush to any conclusion.

The painting contains a tiny inscription "Bunka 2" (1805), so it is likely that at least the preliminary sketches were completed that year. The work might have been finished somewhat later, but certainly not by much.

In March 1806, the Great Bunka Fire burned more than 530 residential quarters in Edo, completely destroying the Nihonbashi area depicted in this scroll. The almost obsessive particularity with which *Kidai Shōran* shows the rows of shops in architectural detail—including their signboards, shop curtains, and interiors—thankfully preserves a record of the city center before it went up in flames.

Fūzoku zukan (Genre scenes), by Hishikawa Moronobu. (TNM Image Archives)

Edo fūzoku zukan (Almanac of Edo scenery), foreword by Santō Kyōden. (Hosomi Museum)

Who commissioned the scroll, and why?

Another outstanding question: Who could have conceived of and commissioned such a painting?

The first thing to strike the viewer's eyes is the title, rendered horizontally in large characters. The calligraphy is not signed, but there are two seals. One, a *hakubun-hou-in* with the characters engraved in the negative so that they are white when stamped, reads "Sajun no in"; the other, with the characters carved so that they show the red seal paste when stamped, reads "Tōshū." One wonders why the calligrapher would not have signed his name.

Together, the two seals lead us to the calligrapher Sano Tōshū, who was active in Edo at the time. His date of birth is unknown, but he died on March 10, 1814. His given name was Jun.

By coincidence, I work as a member of the Chiyoda Ward Commission for Protection of Cultural Properties at Tokyo's Hie Shrine, known in the Tokugawa period as Sannō Shrine. I was quite familiar with a large framed calligraphy in the shrine, as it was a frequent candidate for consideration by our committee (and was in fact named a Ward Cultural Property in 2003). To the left of the large characters is the calligrapher's signature, Tōshū Sajun haisho (signed Tōshū Sajun), along with his seal, reading "Sajun shiin" (personal seal of Sajun). When I saw the title calligraphy in *Kidai Shōran*, I had no doubt it was done by the same person. As it happens, the shrine calligraphy is dated on the back: January, 1805. I can only marvel at my good fortune in encountering another work from the same calligrapher dating from the same time as *Kidai Shōran*.

Framed calligraphy:
Sannō daigongen.
(Hie Shrine, Tokyo)

Calligrapher's seal and date on the framed calligraphy *Sannō daigongen.* (Hie Shrine, Tokyo)

Sano Tōshū was a well-known professional calligrapher in Edo. The connection between him and the scroll's artist is less apparent, but there are some leads. Lacking an heir, at some point between 1804 and 1806 he adopted Santō Kyōzan (1769–1858), who was the younger brother of the writer Santō Kyōden (1761–1816). The elder brother was a first-rate writer of popular *gesaku* fiction who also painted in ukiyo-e style under the name Kitao Masanobu. He was a leading student of contemporary society and mores, and was known for his interest in the study of ancient texts.

In 1798, Kyōden published a two-volume picture book entitled *Shiki no yukikai* (The changing seasons) describing Edo street scenes in words and pictures, with drawings by his teacher, Kitao Shigemasa (1739–1820). Ten years later, he conceived and produced a picture scroll showing twenty-six men and women of various types living in Edo, called *Edo fūzoku zukan* (Almanac of Edo Scenery), paintings by Utagawa Toyokuni (Hosomi Museum, Kyoto). In the foreword to the latter, Kyōden wrote that he expected his realistic depictions of the people to be a source of information for "people a hundred years from now." That is exactly the purpose that *Kidai Shōran* serves, documenting for us a now-lost quarter of the city and the lives of its inhabitants, not one hundred but two hundred years on. Given Kyōden's close connection with the calligrapher Sano Tōshū, one is tempted to conclude that the former may at least have planned the painting.

Tōshū signed the shrine calligraphy, so why didn't he sign the title of the scroll painting, too? The explanation lies in the signature seal he used. The *kanbun* text inscribed on the seal indicates that the completion of the "*ten*" volume was "an urgent matter made at the request of a great man." The wording seems be a quotation, and I have not identified the source, although a similar phrase appears in the *Book of Han*. But it seems possible that an unnamed high-ranking samurai ordered the painting and calligraphy—someone even further in the background than Santō Kyōden. The calligrapher may have refrained from signing his name in deference to that man.

At the time of the scroll's creation at the beginning of the nineteenth century, the rule of the Tokugawa shogunate was peaceful, and the city of Edo was bursting with prosperity and optimism. Someone ordered an artist to paint a scrupulously realistic street scene and also ordered a calligrapher to compose the title. Perhaps it was a daimyō, a vassal of the shogun, or some other high-ranking samurai connected to the shogunate who gave the order, eager to learn about the lives and customs of the common people in minute detail.

Many points regarding this scroll painting remain to be clarified, including, above all, the whereabouts of the missing volume or volumes. The day when I can deliver definitive answers to Professor Ehmcke and Dr. Veit still lies ahead. We can only hope that the publication of this book helps in our search.

Edo fūzoku zukan (Almanac of Edo scenery), foreword by Santō Kyōden. (Hosomi Museum)

Shiki no yukikai (The changing seasons), text by Santō Kyōden, drawings by Kitao Shigemasa. (National Diet Library)

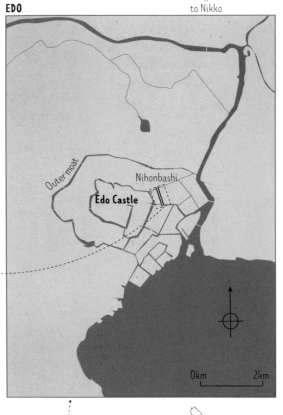

EDO

to Nikko

Outer moat

Nihonbashi

Edo Castle

0km   2km

JAPAN

Edo

The Location of the *Kidai Shōran* Scroll

Top to bottom:
(L) Meiji-era (1868-1912) woodblock print: Nihonbashi Bridge, Telegraph Station, from *Tōkaidō meisho kaisei 53 eki kaisei dōchuki* (Newly edited travel record of famous places on the 53 stages of the Tōkaidō) by Utagawa Hiroshige III. (Tokyo Metropolitan Foundation for History and Culture Image Archives)

(R) Edo-period (1603-1868) woodblock print: *The Tōkaidō, Nihonbashi* by Utagawa Kunisada. (Tokyo Metropolitan Foundation for History and Culture Image Archives)

Meiji-era postcard: *In commemoration of the formal opening of Nihonbashi Bridge: the newly opened Nihonbashi Bridge.* (Tokyo Metropolitan Foundation for History and Culture Image Archives)

Taishō-era (1912-1926) woodblock print: *A Bustling Scene of Nihonbashi Bridge* by Tsuchiya Den. (Tokyo Metropolitan Foundation for History and Culture Image Archives)

Shōwa-era (1926-1989) woodblock print: *Nihonbashi Bridge, Night* by Kawase Hasui. (Tokyo Metropolitan Foundation for History and Culture Image Archives)

Heisei-era (1989-2019) photo: Nihonbashi Bridge today. (Ozawa Hiromu)

A Timeline of Nihonbashi Bridge

1603   After Tokugawa Ieyasu established the shogunate rule in Edo, Nihonbashi Bridge was built as the starting point for Japan's five great trunk roads.

1606   Official noticeboards were placed on Nihonbashi Bridge.

1616   The bridge was reconstructed, with a new configuration 68.5 meters long and 8 meters across.

1657   Nihonbashi was destroyed in the Great Fire of Meireki. According to legend, the fire was started by a priest burning a cursed kimono.

1683   Nihonbashi was destroyed in the Yaoya Oshichi Fire. In 1682, Oshichi, a grocer's daughter, fell in love while taking refuge during a fire. She started another fire the following year in hopes of reuniting with the young man.

In all, the bridge burned down nine times and twice was partially destroyed by fire, but each time was swiftly rebuilt and restored with the shogun's encouragement.

1868   The Tokugawa shogunate ended and the Meiji era began.

1873   The old bridge was replaced with a Western-style bridge 51 meters long and 11 meters across.

1874   Pedestrian walkways were added to the bridge.

1875   Gas lamps were added to the bridge.

1911   The bridge was rebuilt in its modern form. Designed by Tsumaki Yorinaka, it is now a twin arch bridge made of stone, 49 meters long and 27 meters across. The roadway is 18 meters wide, and the walkways are 4.5 meters wide on either side. The railings are decorated with British-style bronze ornaments. The reconstruction cost 500 million yen (US$4.6 million at today's exchange rates, but worth much more at the time).

NIHONBASHI

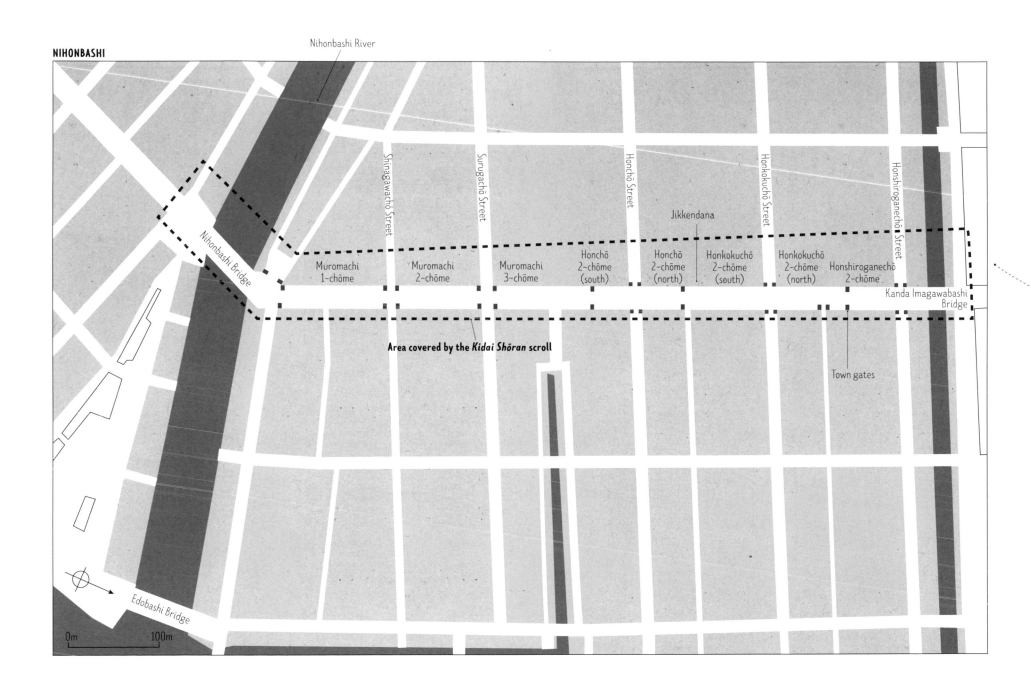

Nihonbashi River

Shinagawachō Street

Surugachō Street

Honchō Street

Honkokuchō Street

Honshiroganechō Street

Jikkendana

Nihonbashi Bridge

Muromachi
1-chōme

Muromachi
2-chōme

Muromachi
3-chōme

Honchō
2-chōme
(south)

Honchō
2-chōme
(north)

Honkokuchō
2-chōme
(south)

Honkokuchō
2-chōme
(north)

Honshiroganechō
2-chōme

Kanda Imagawabashi
Bridge

Area covered by the *Kidai Shōran* scroll

Town gates

Edobashi Bridge

0m   100m

Ozawa Hiromu received a Master's Degree in Literature from the Graduate School of Arts and Letters, Meiji University, and later completed his doctorate. He is a professor of Japanese and Japanese Culture at Chofu Gakuen Junior College. He is currently a professor and director at the Research Center of Edo-Tokyo Urban History at the Edo-Tokyo Museum, focusing on Japanese culture and Japanese art history. He is the author of many books, including *Toshizu no keifu to Edo* (Yoshikawa Koubunkan, 2002) and the co-author of *Bijuaru waido Edo jidai kan* (Visual wide: The Edo period, Shogakukan, 2002).

Kobayashi Tadashi received a Master's Degree in Art History from the Graduate School of Humanities, the University of Tokyo. He was formerly a professor, the Faculty of Letters, Gakushuin University. He is now director at the Okada Museum of Art. His research subjects are centered around Japanese art history. Books he has authored include *Ukiyo-e: Great Japanese Art* (Kodansha USA, 1982), *Utamaro: Portraits from the Floating World* (Kodansha USA, 2001), *Hokusai no bijin* (Shogakukan, 2005), *Nihon suibokuga zenshi* (The history of Japanese ink painting, Kodansha, 2018) and *Ukiyoe* (Yamakawa Shuppansha, 2019).

Juliet Winters Carpenter is a prolific translator who studied at the University of Michigan, and lived in Japan for over 45 years. She received the Japan-US Friendship Commission Prize for the Translation of Japanese Literature in 1980 for *Secret Rendezvous* by Abe Kobo and again in 2014 for *A True Novel* by Mizumura Minae. Her previous Japan Library translations include Isoda Michifumi's *Unsung Heroes of Old Japan* (2017) and Nakano Koji's *Words to Live by* (2018). She lives on Whidbey Island in Washington.

About the
Translator

to ← Nihonbashi Bridge

From → Imagawabashi Bridge, Kanda

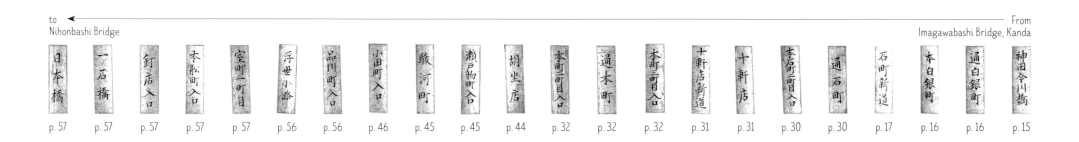

日本橋	一石橋	釘店入口	本舩町入口	室町一町目	浮世小路	品川町入口	小田町入口	駿河町	瀬戸物町入口	胡坐店	本町二町目入口	通本町	本町三町目入口	十軒店新道	十軒店	本石町三町目入口	通石町	石町新道	本白銀町	通白銀町	神田今川橋
p. 57	p. 57	p. 57	p. 57	p. 57	p. 56	p. 56	p. 46	p. 45	p. 45	p. 44	p. 32	p. 32	p. 32	p. 31	p. 31	p. 30	p. 30	p. 17	p. 16	p. 16	p. 15

（英文版）『熙代勝覧』の日本橋　活気にあふれた江戸の町
The Kidai Shōran *Scroll: Tokyo Street Life in the Edo Period*

2020 年 3 月 27 日　第 1 刷発行

著　者　小澤弘・小林忠
訳　者　ジュリエット・ウィンターズ・カーペンター
発行所　一般財団法人　出版文化産業振興財団
　　　　〒 101-0051　東京都千代田区神田神保町 2-2-30
　　　　電話　03-5211-7283
ホームページ　https://www.jpic.or.jp/

印刷・製本所　大日本印刷株式会社

This book has been produced "backwards" for a very important reason.

Japanese has traditionally been written vertically from right to left, and the *Kidai Shōran* scroll—the artistic masterpiece that is the subject of this book—was also created to be viewed in that direction. Rather than "reverse engineer" the experience of viewing this scroll for readers, this English translation follows in the footsteps of the Japanese original, and should be read from right to left.